AA
Aux Arc Publication
(Ozark Publication)

DAM
Over Troubled Waters

robert dean anderson

Copyright 2014 by Robert Dean Anderson

All rights reserved, including the right to reproduce this book or portions thereof in any form whatsoever without written permission from the author.
robert.dean.anderson@gmail.com

ISBN-13-978-0-9720680-0-0
First Edition
Printed July 2014
in the USA

This book is dedicated to the men and women who built
their bridge over troubled waters and created
which was at the time the
largest man-made lake in the world.

RALPH WOOD STREET.
Age 27

INTRODUCTION:

The "War of the Currents" between Thomas Edison's direct current DC dynamos and Nikola Tesla's alternating current AC polyphase technology ended when George Westinghouse successfully completed the Niagara Falls project using Tesla's patents and inventions which Westinghouse had purchased. When Westinghouse was able to transport electrical power over great distances by stepping the AC voltages up to compensate for losses in the transmission lines, then stepping the voltages down at the point of use, the central electrical power plant was born.

    The Niagara Falls generating station led to the widespread idea of using the power of moving water to drive the generators for those central electrical plants. Water's power had been demonstrated from ancient practices of water-driven mills, water wheels, etc. to be a valuable source of unharnessed energy. Entrepreneurs and investors jumped at the chance to get involved in one of the new technologies of the time. Ralph Wood Street, a St. Joseph, Missouri lawyer, was one such visionary. In 1912, Street was forming the idea of using the power of moving water to generate electricity for sale. And in Missouri there was an abundance of moving water. Street's idea led to the construction of Bagnell Dam nearly twenty years later.

    Many twists would be turned before actual construction of the dam. Events and actions centered around three people. There was the dreamer, Ralph Street, who devoted twenty years of life into realizing his dream of providing electrical power from moving water. And, there was the schemer, Walter Cravens, whose name was spoken on the floor of Congress and appeared on the desk of the President of the United States, but his manipulations brought the project to a halt. Lastly, Alice B. Todd, the lady banker who rose to heights in the management of land banks that only one other woman had attained, but her devotion to the wrong man was costly.

Two Federal laws would come to figure prominently in the plans and strategies used by the promoters and the builders, the Federal Farm Loan Act of 1916 and the Federal Water Power Act of 1920. There would be four federal grand juries, five criminal trials, numerous appeals to the Federal Circuit Court of Appeals, one local Missouri Circuit Court hearing, the conviction of three people involved, three failed federally chartered land banks, dissension among county court members, 180 land condemnation suits and the innundation of a complete town of 400 plus people who stood by to watch their homes and businesses burned to make way for the country's largest man-made lake..

Some called it, "The engineering feat of its day." At the time construction started, the engineering designers said it was part of the single largest electrical power contract ever entered into and claimed it would be the largest project on the continent. It came at the beginning of the Great Depression and the builders said 20,000 people were employed overall. Supporters bragged that it would create the world's largest man-made lake. Records indicate that nearly 2000 property owners were displaced. After completion, analysts said it had been the largest privately financed dam in this country and predicted accurately that it would be the last. Little wonder.

But the real wonder of the project belongs to one man's tenacity who never gave up a dream and to the 13,000 individuals who did with their hands with small help from power equipment in less that 24 months what would take years today.

THE DREAMER

LED BY A DREAM, Ralph Wood Street stepped off the Missouri Pacific branch line railcar into a blustery, cold February morning. This was Bagnell, Missouri, a place he'd been before. Five months earlier, September 1923, he had taken his first active steps to realize that long held dream. A dream that would produce electricity and produce it with the power of flowing water.

"Possibly that first occurred in 1912," he said to others about his dream.

Accompanied on the previous trip by a Kansas City contractor named Bickel and an electrical engineer, Walter Eyssell, Street had completed a preliminary reconnaissance survey by measuring the discharge of the Osage River that ran beside Bagnell, inspecting possible dam sites, inquiring into land values and investigating geological conditions of the area. Bickel was again with him on this trip to offer his judgment on likely spots to locate a dam.

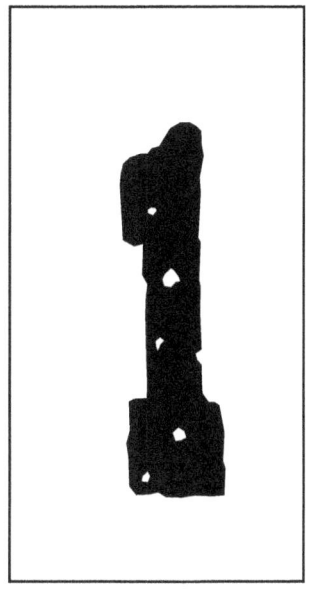

Bagnell wasn't much of a town. The area was south of the Missouri River, north of the Ozark mountains, in a section of the state rifted by streams and rivers draining toward the Missouri and ultimately into the Mississippi near St. Louis. The area was sparsely populated with poor, rocky soil except for the rich alluvial deposits along the rivers such as the Osage.

The region had first been populated by several native American tribes, the Osage being the largest. The first of the Europeans into the area were the French trappers who gave names to settlements, even the Ozarks themselves (*Aux Arc*s, Land of the Bows, a referral to the unbreakable bows the Osage carried that were fashioned from the indestructible Osage Orange tree). The trappers were followed by miners looking for mineral deposits that were few, then the woodsmen to harvest the plentiful forests of hardwood.

Now, here was Street to capitalize on one of the last natural resources of the area to be exploited—the flowing waters.

Bagnell had been named after a man who did work for the spur line of the Missouri Pacific Railroad that was extended from Missouri's capitol, Jefferson City, to transport railroad ties. At the close of the century people called Bagnell the railroad tie capitol of the country. A major industry in this part of the state, it consisted of individuals hacking out ties from the native forest of abundant hardwoods at a dime apiece and floating them down the Osage to Bagnell where they were loaded onto railcars and shipped throughout the nation. But the tie business had died and the town threatened to follow.

The closest bridge across the Osage River was miles upstream. A ferry operated in Bagnell to take the party across if they desired. A blacksmith shop, a restaurant and a hotel pretty much made up the town.

Street needed a mode of transportation and a guide to help them get around. A local citizen, Homer Houston, offered his services and said he could obtain a team of horses and a light wagon. Along with Bickel, Street was accompanied by the head of the Geology Department at the University of Missouri in Columbia, Dr. E.B. Branson, to help in selecting the best location for a dam. Branson would look at three tentative sites and with his knowledge, help determine the best site that would offer acceptable water tightness and rock formations to provide a base for the necessary structure.

Street, born in St. Joseph, Missouri, graduated, not as an engineer, but from the law school at the University of Michigan and began his law practice in 1909 in St. Joseph. He became a partner with the firm, Gutherie, Campbell and Street and moved with his practice to Kansas City in 1915. In 1918 he began taking on large companies as clients and dealing in the sale of bonds. This would later put him in the same business circle as Walter Price Cravens who was promoting bonds for a newly chartered federal joint stock land bank.

Street's idea of establishing an electrical power plant in central Missouri with its abundance of rushing waters immediately caught Cravens' interest. His bank could help Street in his financial support needed for the plan. Where Street saw electricity resulting from his dream, Cravens saw dollars. They struck a deal.

Street was not the first to recognize the potential of converting the state's enormous amount of moving water providing energy that could be converted into the production of electrical power. Following the opening of the nation's first hydroelectric power plant in Grand Rapids, Michigan in 1882, a power plant was constructed in Grand Falls, Missouri in 1890 to supply electrical power to area mines in Southwest Missouri. The Captains of Industry created a huge demand for electricity and governments and private enterprise scrambled to meet that need.

The Kansas City market that Street had his eye on, waited for a central provider of electrical power. City streets were webbed, like most municipalities at the time, with a maze of electrical transmission lines serving mostly adjoining localities with DC (direct current) power for lighting. Kansas City Power & Light Company, the company that came to provide most of the city's electricity, had just emerged in 1922 from a series of takeovers, buyouts, spinoffs and bankruptcies among companies providing power for trolleys and lighting. The company, which traced its roots to 1881 when Joseph S. Chick purchased the exclusive Jackson County, Missouri and Wyandotte County, Kansas rights for the Thompson-Houston arc lighting system, was looking for providers of electrical power.

Street's dream remained just that until the passage in 1920 of the Federal Water Power Act. Now, there was legal authority and a means of obtaining financial assistance for such projects. It was time for Street to convert his dream into reality.

"I began to study the Act with a view of becoming familiar with the requirements and began to gather data regarding it," Street said. "I discovered that a man by the name of Banks had applied for a preliminary permit and the government had granted a preliminary permit which continued in effect for about two years and expired in 1923. He had a scheme of 'bank high' dams and was going to tunnel through some big necks in the river, divert the water through the necks and generate power in that manner."

The river in Banks' plan, the Osage, originates in Kansas where the Marais des Cygnes (French for "Marsh of Swans," presumably named after the trumpeter swans that frequented the area, locals say *mare dey sein*;) flows into the state of Missouri and joins the Little Osage River. The Osage ends at the Missouri River a few miles downstream from Missouri's capitol of Jefferson City

The plan by W.R. Banks of Lamar, Missouri, called for a diversion dam 30 to 40 feet high on the Osage near the mouth of the Niangua River. The project would have created a tunnel 8000 feet long across the neck of the river bend below a place called Hurricane Deck. Another dam at that point would house the power wheels. The permit, issued for 50 years, required Banks to design a series of locks to allow river traffic around the dams and to determine the stage and available flow of the Osage making certain the water level below Warsaw, Missouri would not decline.

Street watched closely the results in 1922 of that plan and read the reports from the U.S. Engineers' office as well reports about other projects that had been proposed in the past, none of which had been completed.

Street said about Bank's plan, "It was canceled out in July, 1923, because he was unable to carry on his work and show that he had an economical plan. I secured access to the reports which they (the U.S. Engineers) had made and they reported adversely upon the economics of Bank's project on the ground that he could not develop power economically by any such plan as that."

Street went on to do a complete study of the reports on the "bank high" dam concept such as Banks' and reached the conclusion that, in addition to being economically unfeasible, technically that method of producing electricity was also not possible on the mercurial Osage River. That prompted his September 1923 trip to Bagnell.

"We made the discharge measurements of the Osage River that were available since about 1892," he said of the trip. "We made a full study to determine whether a hydro electric project would be possible."

Street was now thinking about a different type of electrical generating plant. One that would cost much more than Banks' plan, but would deliver power far in excess of anything heard of or talked about in the past. From his studies he found the fluctuation of the Osage to be from 142,000 cubic feet per second at flood stage to a low water flow of 325 cubic feet per second.

"Considering the character of the stream, it was necessary to regulate the flow of the stream by a large reservoir," he said.

Banks' plan for a potential source of electrical power demonstrated the interest in the Osage. Sometime during that year Street convinced Cravens that a storage type of facility was the way to go.

Street obtained maps from the United States Geological Service, mounted them on linen and joined the sections of the river together. He traced out a 650 foot contour for the reservoir, combined that with a stream flow-study and a power outlet study and after a month or more of preparation, he made an application for a temporary permit from the Federal Power Commission in December, 1923.

After his three-week winter trek in the field that year, Street's next move was to employ the Burns and McDonnell Engineering firm that had started in Kansas City in 1898 and concentrated on sewer and water projects, but also built some smaller hydro plants.

"We employed them to make a survey of the reservoir area in order to determine the contents and also for a basis of the land or ownership of the land inundated by the Osage Project," Street said.

They gave him an estimate of the area that would be affected and mapped the area that would be covered by the reservoir the dam would create. They put their first crew of 25 in the field in March 1924, and completed their task in September of that year. For their surveying work they were paid $40,438.90 ($491,332.64), [*NOTE: figures in parenthesis would be the equivalent, current value at time of publication*]. A net head, or distance from the top of the water level on the high side of the dam to the water level on the low side of 100 feet and a surface elevation of 655 feet above the sea level at Biloxi, MS, were used for the map the firm created.

It was significant that Street now spoke in terms of "WE" instead of "I," indicating Cravens had entered the picture. Walter Cravens said in fact, that it was Clinton Burns of Burns and McDonnell who convinced him of the feasibility of Street's plan.

Street also had kept a close eye on two rapidly flowing rivers in the southeastern part of the state. The Western Tie and Timber Company of St. Louis had already, in 1921, been granted a permit to "make necessary engineering investigations …to make full practicable utilization of power possibilities of the site." Street's plan for supplying electrical power to Kansas City and St. Louis tentatively included projects on the Current and two on the Eleven Point River.

Time became crucial for Street and his projects.

The major requirements for a plan of the scope he had in mind on the rivers of Missouri fell into three categories: funding first, land acquisition next, then construction.

The actual construction of the dam, including the cost and necessary funding, would depend on the site chosen. That's why Street was there in Bagnell during that blustery February, 1924. The site for a potential dam and resulting reservoir depended on topography and surface condition primarily. Street with his maps, stream flows, topography studies and the advice of Dr. Branson, Bickel and others, selected a potential site about four miles upstream of the town of Bagnell that had a projecting point on the southwest side of the river and a steeply sloping ridge on the northeast side. The valley stretched between them a half-mile in width, generally narrower, according to his maps, than the average width of the flood plain in the river's path. The bedrock at this point was promising, but required further investigation.

J.E. Gehrean was sent out to ascertain the ownership of the land in the area Burns and McDonnell said would be under water. Gehrean was able to do that by taking the maps created to abstractors in the affected counties, Camden, Miller, Morgan and Benton during that summer and into the fall.

In July 1924, the Federal Power Commission rejected Street's application for a temporary permit to build the dam on the Osage River.

"I made a more complete form of records of the river and an argument in support of the economics of the development," Street said. "Evidently they had the reports of the other engineers and they could not get it out of their system that this was on an entirely different basis, and with the additional information and data, they granted the permit."

The Federal Power Commission granted the permit November 12, 1924. The permit, however, was in Walter Cravens' name. The agreement between Street and Cravens at this point, evidently, was that Street would do the work and Cravens would supply the money. And to provide collateral for the money, Cravens was putting everything in his name. In a petition filed with the Public Service Commission of Missouri, some of the details of the agreement were expressed as a contract between the Missouri Hydro Electric Power Company—a company that Street and Cravens created—and Walter Cravens wherein Cravens obligated himself to, "assign and transfer to applicant the license when and as procured from the Federal Power Commission without compensation to him nor other consideration than the reimbursement of the actual out-of-pocket expenditures made by him in the doing of the preliminary work and procuring of the permit."

"We prepared a form of option and began to undertake to get the options from the people in the valley on their land," Street recalled. "That work was started in December, 1924, and carried on vigorously and at the end we had seven or eight parties out in the field and we had options on something like 50,000 acres of land."

Gehrean employed W.O. Esther of Linn Creek, E.H. Boeschen of Versailles and the same Homer Houston of Bagnell who had driven Street and his party around earlier, along with the seven or eight crews to contact the owners of the parcels of land that would be under water.

Landowners were offered five dollars for an option to buy the land at a proposed price or let the property go into condemnation. To some of the property owners it looked like a good deal, to others it was a threat, "Take our offer or we'll take your property anyway." It was the Federal Water Power Act of 1920 that would give the dam builders the legal right to do that through eminent domain. Purchase of the affected land, or legal options to buy it, were necessary before any banks could be expected to put funds into the operation. According to Street the company put the 50,000 acres of land under option in the four counties with agreeable property owners, but, he emphasized, the company never actually purchased any of the land before the options expired.

During the spring of 1925, Missouri state geologist, Dr. H.A. Buehler assisted by Dr. Dake from the Rolla School of Mines, investigated the reservoir site for soundness and water-tightness. To complete the plan for subsurface exploration, Dr. Buehler recommended core drilling the site so Street hired Sprague and Henwood, Inc. of Scranton, PA. They conducted diamond drill borings consisting of 41 two and three inch diameter holes in a double row along the heel and toe of the dam, a single row of holes along the dam site and an oblique row of holes on either side and end of the dam to establish a suitable foundation for a minimum of 30 feet below the existing water surface. One hole in the center was drilled to a depth of 342 feet. They were paid $22,451.75 ($272,788.76).

The core drilling that Street paid for established that the bedrock was Gasconade dolomite limestone overlying a comparatively thin horizontal layer of Gunter Sandstone beneath which—to a depth of at least 240 feet—was Proctor dolomite limestone. Sandstones have a wide range of strength depending largely upon the amount and type of cement matrix material occupying the voids, or "vugs" in the rock. Dolomite is a calcium, magnesium carbonate of varying proportions that includes white marble when in the crystalline form. The strata, they found to their satisfaction, to be practically horizontal, lessening the chances of uplifting forces under the structure. The dolomite, which largely predominated, was solid and would weather well.

The cavities in some of the strata of sandstone gave the appearance of porosity, but actually did not interconnect and were therefore doubtful that water would pass through them. Hydraulic pressure tests were performed to determine the tightness and character of the rock foundation. Grouting in the foundation would sufficiently guard against percolation. The bearing values of the dolomite and the Gunter sandstone were found to be satisfactory.

The 5300 feet of core drillings and all the tests proved the soundness of the rock formations to the engineers. The foundation would carry the weight of the structure.

Cleveland Aerial Surveys was contracted to photograph the area. Immediately following the aerial photography, the Charles B. Hawley Engineering Company of Washington came onto the scene to check the site at the 650 foot contour and did a double line of levels to check the accuracy of Burns and McDonnell's survey. The Hawley Company was brought in at the suggestion of the E.H. Rollins and Sons bankers as a requirement to consider financing the project. Hawley's report, like the core drilling, was favorable. The bankers were now interested in working on the Osage River Dam project.

The Hawley Company's report that was released in October 1925, found that a head of 95 feet was economical and could possibly be increased to 100 feet without creating a flood hazard to the lower portions of the town of Warsaw in Benton County. They based their design on a primary and secondary power output of 350,000,000 kilowatt-hours per year and if the elevation was increased from 655 to 660, an additional 25,000,000 kwh was possible. Hawley put a construction cost at $13,400,000 ($162,810,000) on a design with 20 spillway gates to discharge a maximum flood stage.

Street had already begun the application for the Missouri Hydro Electric Power Company to be incorporated. Incorporation was granted November 24, 1924 with Walter Cravens listed as president, Walter Eyssell as secretary and Ralph Street as vice president. Five hundred shares of common stock were authorized with 498 shares going to Cravens and one share each to Eyssell and Street.

Street had given up his law practice by this time and devoted all of his efforts in developing the dam. Without an income. It was not until June 1925, when the following resolution was adopted and entered in the minutes of the board of directors of the Hydro company, did Street see any rewards from his efforts:

"Whereas R.W. Street has, since the first of January, 1925, been devoting a substantial part of his time to the affairs of the company and since May 1, 1925, has been devoting substantially all of his time to the interest of the company, therefore, be it resolved that payments to R.W. Street of a salary of $500 per month from January 1, 1925, to May 1, 1925, a salary be fixed at $800 per month until further orders of the board."

It was in the fall of 1925, Street said, that, "We asked the commission (Public Service Commission of Missouri) to hear us informally and we discussed the plans and talked the situation over with the commission."

Here's how Street would later describe the work done that summer and fall to the commissioners on the Public Service Commission: "It was absolutely essential—nobody would build a dam down there if this was not done. We have had the Cement Association loan a man that we put on the payroll to take charge of making the tests of the gravel and various materials, and that is one of the reasons why this can be built for the small amount of money is the fact that the gravel is right there at the dam site, and a very large amount of it will be recovered in excavating for the foot of the dam, and they took samples and sent it to the laboratories at Chicago, and they made all the various tests to determine whether it was suitable for the concrete. We sunk test holes with a cubic foot orange peel bucket clear across the river for the purpose of obtaining samples of the materials tested, and every group of bankers that we negotiated with have had their engineers out there, for all of them wanted to make an actual physical investigation of the situation."

Street was busy at the construction site throughout 1924 and 1925. Cravens was supplying the money that came, as far as Street knew, from proceeds of Cravens' Kansas City Joint Stock Land Bank and the finance company Cravens had started. After all, the checks were all signed by the secretary of the bank, Alice B. Todd, an attractive woman who had come from Salina, Kansas, with Cravens.

As many as 365 men were at work at the site chosen for the dam. The Bickel Contracting Company of Kansas City completed a bunkhouse, three foremen's cottages, a mess hall capable of serving 450 men, a kitchen that could serve 900 men, a headquarters building for office purposes, a headquarters dormitory for visitors, a permanent dormitory, a waterworks system, sewage and an electrical plant either completed or under construction A gravel road from Highway Number 54 at Bagnell to the dam site was built. One branch of the road went to the upper camp on the eastern bluff and the other to the lower camp in the flood land of the river.

A standard gauge railroad was being extended from the Bagnell Branch line of the Missouri Pacific to the Osage River near the dam site. So far, Street had expended $55,232.05 on the gravel road and the railroad to establish the embankments, bridges and culverts including a $15,000 bridge over the Little Gravois Creek. Nearly two miles of track was laid up to, but not across the Osage.

One of the interested financiers Cravens had brought into the project was Guy Huston, a self-proclaimed authority on farm finances. Huston had offices in Chicago and New York, was president of the Chicago Joint-Stock Land Bank, vice president of the Pickrel Walnut Company of St. Louis and a director of the Southern Minnesota Joint-Stock Land Bank. Huston visited the Bagnell site and was impressed enough to agree to advance up to $600,000 for construction and to promote a $15 million bond sale.

Planning of the dam, land acquisition and funding were aligned for a successful beginning. But, storm clouds loomed on the horizon. Word was spreading throughout the area about the plan for a massive dam. People in Warsaw, county seat of Benton County and located on the banks of the Osage, worried about possible flooding in their town. The people of Linn Creek, a town of about 500 and the county seat of Camden County were stirring, waking to the fact that their town lay smack in the middle of the proposed lake. And some of the townspeople were not content with the idea, especially J.W. Vincent, publisher of the *Reveille* newspaper and a member of the Missouri Legislature.

Before any actual construction could begin on the dam itself, approval for the project was needed from both the Federal Power Commission and the Missouri State Public Service Commission. Since July 1924, Cravens had in hand a permit from the Federal Power Commission in his name, but the last barrier was the State of Missouri. That's when the local opposition was expected to surface. On December 12, 1925, Ralph Street signed an application to the Missouri Public Service Commission for a Certificate of Public Convenience and Necessity for the Missouri Hydro-Electric Power Company.

"After starting this," Street told, "we then started and received a considerable amount of encouragement from a group of bankers . . . we made a temporary contract with this group of bankers and with Gardner S. Williams, a hydraulic engineer on the University of Michigan selected by Howe, Snow and Bertles and E.H. Rollins (bankers), and I spent a week or ten days more in Kansas City going over the project with him, and he made a careful investigation of the whole situation . . . he made a trip over the project from Bagnell to Warsaw and we gave him all the data we had collected and on the strength of it and the tentative setup with the bankers, we filed for the approval of something like $20,000,000 ($243,000,000) in securities with the commission (Case 4633) and Mr. Williams after making a month's study . . . from the time they took the matter up it meant more than a month or six weeks before we could get an answer from the ones it was submitted to, but he made a favorable report but by the time the favorable report was made the government had started an investigation of Guy Huston and others interested with Guy Huston and so they dropped it. The others became alarmed. In December we stopped all work there at the dam site."

The Public Service Commission had set a public hearing (Case 4232) to consider the application for December 23, 1925. The opposition Street and Cravens hoped to pacify and win over, lined up at the Commission's door. The battle was on. Street, however, was elsewhere, financial backing having taken a sharp turn for the worse. The checks from Alice B. Todd had stopped.

WALTER CRAVENS

THE SCHEMER

YOUNG WALTER CRAVENS grew up around his father's insurance and mortgage business in Salina, Kansas. The elder Cravens, Richard Price (Dick) Cravens, a law graduate of the University of Missouri, had been born in a log cabin in Ray County, Missouri. He moved to Salina, Kansas in 1878 and after one year of law practice there he started an insurance business in Salina and founded the Cravens Mortgage Company in 1909. He served for three years as president of the Kansas State Association of Local Insurance Agents and was well regarded in that business. Walter attended schools in Salina and after a stint with the H.D. Lee Mercantile Company, joined his father in the mortgage business.

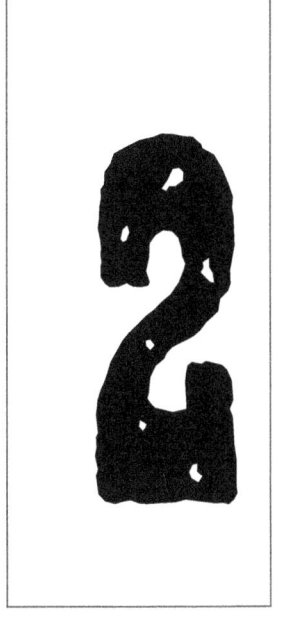

The father's business was prosperous but Walter didn't talk in thousands of dollars when he talked of his aspirations. He talked in millions. While Ralph Street's dreams and plans were of dams and electrical energy, Walter Cravens was dreaming of an empire.

When Congress passed the Federal Farm Loan Act on 17 July 1916, that was the opportunity Walter had been looking for. Farms were becoming mechanized and farmers needed to borrow money to obtain the newfangled farm equipment. Private banks were less interested in making these loans because of the reliance on the success of harvests to pay them back. The Farm Loan Act created 12 chartered Land Banks throughout the country and established joint-stock land banks that were financed through private capital and were permitted to make loans in the states in which they were chartered and in one contiguous state. These banks catered to farmers who wanted loans in excess of $10,000, which was the maximum amount federal land banks were allowed to loan. In addition, the joint-stock land banks could make loans to others engaged in agriculture besides those who actually tilled the soil.

About 87 joint-stock land banks were chartered before 1920, but only about 30 were in fact opened for business.

The joint-stock land bank was where Walter, now a partner with his father in the mortgage company, saw the greatest opportunities. The Cravens Mortgage Company was already doing a fairly extensive farm loan business. But not in the larger millions Walter always talked about. In the very next year after the Farm Loan Act passed, he founded the Liberty Joint Stock Land Bank in 1917 in Salina, the fifth such bank to receive a charter and the third to commence business.

Walter was known as the "bond man," for the mortgage company. The mortgage company borrowed money from banks to buy stock in Cravens' new land bank. The mortgage company had guaranteed the farm mortgages that it sold to various life insurance companies. At the beginning of the land bank, the mortgage company had been compelled to buy back a large number of defaulted mortgages. Walter's new joint stock land bank promptly made new loans on the defaulted mortgages. Between June 1, 1918 and December 1, 1921, fifty-two such mortgages totaling $225,500 ($2,739,825) were transferred from the mortgage company to the land bank. The mortgage company used the proceeds from the sale of the mortgages to pay off the loans made to buy the land bank stock.

Cravens moved the bank to Kansas City in December, 1922 and changed the name to the Kansas City Joint Stock Land Bank The bank had $10,000,000 ($121,500,000) in farm mortgages on the books at the time. Thanks to the rapidly increasing agricultural economy in the years following World War 1, and to Cravens' ability, the bank soon had twice the number of loans as any other joint stock land bank in the country. By the beginning of 1927 the mortgages had grown to $50,000,000 on its books. It had about 8000 outstanding loans.

That same year, 1922, when Cravens moved his business to Kansas City, he entered the automobile business. He got into an insolvent auto sales company and when he found himself with a load of unsalable used cars, he began trading them for equities in farm mortgages in Missouri, wrote the mortgages as assets to the automobile company thereby guaranteeing the bank notes outstanding.

With Missouri's law against branch banking, the bank soon outgrew its two-story facilities becoming the second largest Joint-Stock Land Bank in the country. Cravens hired architects Keene and Simpson to design a new building specifically for banking purposes. That building, at 15 West 10th Street in downtown Kansas City's financial district, was based on Italian Renaissance style and was distinctive enough to earn the 1924 Kansas City Business District's Gold Medal. The builder was the same Bickel who accompanied Ralph Street to Bagnell to scout the location of a dam on the Osage River. The building was ultimately placed on the National Register of Historic Places.

Walter Cravens was quick to deploy his financial and entrepreneurial wizardry. Not just president of the Kansas City Joint Stock Land Bank, he was also president of the Missouri Joint Stock Land Bank, vice-president and director of the Safe Deposit Company of Kansas City, director of the Denver Joint Stock Land Bank and director of the American Under-

KANSAS CITY JOINT STOCK LAND BANK AT 15 WEST 10TH STREET

writing Company. By now, the capital stock in the bank had increased from the original $250,000 to $700,000, all of which was issued. Teaming with Guy Huston, with the two swapping ideas and schemes for stock and bond sales of their enterprises, Cravens drove the price of the stock in his joint stock land bank to as high as 180 percent of the initial price.

He formed the Kansas City Finance company and the land bank paid the company $978,533 for the construction of the Land Bank building. The finance company only paid out $696,797 for construction, the difference apparently going into Cravens' pocket..

By 1923, Cravens and Street were another team.

Cravens took Street's idea of building a hydroelectric project to provide electrical power to the cities of St. Louis and Kansas City and shopped it around. He talked with a Mr. Doty of the Foundation Company of New York, the largest construction company in the world. The idea had plausibility. A dam could make money and money was Walter Cravens' quest. Besides, the bubble on farm mortgages, if not bursting, was starting to deflate. Foreclosures were starting to mount. The joint stock land bank was coming into possession of Kansas and Missouri farms at a time when there was a shrinking market for them. The ingenuity of Walter Cravens went to work. If a huge reservoir was to be created by the dam Street talked about, then the land that would be flooded would have to be purchased. And the sellers would need another farm to move to. Why not one of the foreclosed farms?

On March 10, 1925, a contract was entered into between the Missouri Hydro Electric Company and the Kansas City Joint Stock Land Bank wherein the bank, "in the due course of the conduct of its business foreclosed loans and taken over the title to a substantial acreage of land throughout the states of Missouri and Kansas, and is desirous of converting this land into cash, the market for farm land being very depressed . . .and being unable to find purchasers for this land . . . and whereas it now appears that many of the farmers within the area of the (Missouri Hydro Electric Company) project would be willing to trade their farms for such farms (the bank) owns elsewhere . . . the (Hydro) agrees to purchase from (the bank) for cash, as much of the land within the project area as the Bank may acquire by trading. . ."

A bond salesman named Van Meter opened a New York office to sell stocks and bonds in the Kansas City Joint Stock Land Bank. The promotion for the stock implied that the U.S. government stood behind the joint stock land bank and therefore, the investor would assume it to be a no-risk venture. This, of course, was not true. The misleading promotion of the stock turned out to be trouble for both Huston and Cravens.

Cravens next scheme was to gain approval to issue bonds. That's when Street filed the request for case Number 4633 from the Public Service Commission for the issuance of $20,000,000 worth of bonds in the Missouri Hydro Electric Power Company.

Since beginning the joint stock land bank in Salina, Cravens began dealing in millions of dollars just like he had been dreaming about. His dream and Ralph Street's dream were starting to come together. By 1925 Cravens had amassed business assets of five million dollars and would be named one of Kansas City's 100 Foremost Men in a book by Walter P. Tracy in 1925. Tracy praised him for establishing and directing the Joint-Stock Land Bank, which at the time had $35,000,000 in deposits and employed 100 people.

Tracy's book listed Cravens as a Democrat, a Baptist and a 32nd Degree Scottish Rite Mason and Shriner. Listed also were Cravens' membership in the Kansas City Club, the Mission Hills Golf and Country Club, the Automobile Club, Chamber of Commerce and the Real Estate Board. He lived with his wife Bertha and two daughters, Virginia and Frances.

Cravens appeared to be the ideal financier for Ralph Street's Osage River dam project. He provided Street with $1,850,000 in construction money, funneled through the Kansas City Finance Company, in the next several years. With that funding in hand, Street moved constantly to keep the project going.

Three days after the state issued incorporation papers for the Missouri Hydro Electric Power Company, Cravens received a preliminary permit in his name from the Federal Power Commission for Project Number 459MO to begin initial work on the task of, "planning and constructing a dam on the Osage River in the vicinity of Bagnell, Missouri."

The preliminary permit was granted in accordance with the provisions of the Federal Water Power Act. This particular act, in plain terms among other provisions, allowed the government and private enterprises the power of condemnation for the public good. This power provided incentive to the landowners who would be forced to sell or trade their farms. The eminent domain power would be utilized in federal and local courts numerous times before the dam was constructed.

The Cravens' empire was pretty tight. Walter's father, Richard Price Cravens, was listed as chairman of the board of directors of the Kansas City Joint-Stock Land Bank and the Cravens Mortgage Company of Salina, Kansas. Walter's brothers, Richard Harold and Charles Russell were named to the bank's board of directors as were J. B. Smith and Thomas Comerford, both of Salina. Always, four of the directors would be named Cravens. Ralph Street was named vice-president of the bank and the secretary was Alice B. Todd who had come to Kansas City from Salina with Walter Cravens.

From the beginning, Walter Cravens created a cozy relationship among his various companies. When he chartered the Liberty Joint-Stock Land bank in Salina, he began rewarding the Cravens Mortgage Company with a two percent sales commission on all mortgages made in Missouri and Kansas. At that time, it was what was termed a verbal agreement. The commissions were paid whether the loans were made by agents of the mortgage company or by the land bank. In the books on August 30, 1926, $400,173.72 had been paid out in commission to the Finance company with $137,109 still due. The federal farm loan board would later disapprove of the agreement on commissions, but not until after it was continued with the Kansas City Joint-Stock Land Bank.

Checks and money were passed back and forth between the Kansas City Finance Company, which Cravens owned, and the land bank in transactions only Cravens could explain. Alice B. Todd wrote the checks, Cravens signed them. No one else was involved. In 1925 Cravens created the Farmers Fund. Frozen assets in the form of foreclosed mortgages were sold to the Farmers Fund, used to trade for land along the Osage River between the planned dam site and Warsaw, then the value of the land that had been traded for was written back on the books of the land bank.

Cravens and his Land Bank had begun to use the trading agreement between the bank and the hydro company to acquire land in the area of the dam. Foreclosures on mortgages escalated to an alarming rate. By 1925 Cravens' land bank had foreclosed on $1,700,000 in farm mortgages. The value of agricultural land in Missouri and Kansas was practically destroyed by this drop in land prices and made it difficult if not impossible for the land bank to sell off the properties that had been foreclosed on. This was when Cravens devised the plan of dealing with the bad debt or toxic mortgages.

The Farmers Fund Company that Cravens created was the subject Carl Herbert Schwartz covered in his *"Financial Study of the Joint Stock Land Banks: A Chapter in Farm Mortgage Banking,"* writing that, "In order to conceal the true condition of the bank, affiliated companies were organized to take over real estate so that such assets continued to appear as mortgage loans on the bank's books."

Cravens' Farmers Fund Company then began carrying out the trading agreement that had been made between the land bank and the hydro-electric company. Street proclaimed he was not a party to the practice and opposed it. The practice Cravens employed in creating the Farmers Fund and the Missouri-Kansas Farms Company was the same practice Guy Huston used in Minnesota, Chicago and Des Moines, Iowa.

Beginning in 1924 and extending into 1925, the land bank began entering on their books a number of "Straw" loans. These "Straw" loans were actually fictitious loans registered in the name of an irresponsible person for land already acquired by the bank through foreclosure. The fictitious loans were then entered onto the bank's books as new loans replacing the foreclosed loans. Accrued interest on the straw loans was entered on the books as income, although no actual money was involved. Again, Cravens and Miss Todd handled these transactions between them.

In a letter from Cravens to Guy Huston dated October 12, 1925, Cravens wrote: "We have worked out a deal with Bickel for construction work on the hydro project at Bagnell . . .Mr. Bickel is to have a third of the 10 percent profits, the other two-thirds to go to you, Mr. Street and myself...

I am sending this letter to your house as I want you to see it Sunday and also I would rather that it did not go to the office."

It would always be Cravens' contention that he alone conceived the idea for creating a great waterpower project in central Missouri to furnish power to Kansas City and St. Louis and indirectly form a market for the frozen

22 DAM OVER TROUBLED WATERS

POSTER ADVERTISING GUY HUSTON AS A FARM LOAN EXPERT

assets of the land bank in the form of foreclosed mortgages. By shuffling the funds between his various companies and from loans made to him by Guy Huston and banks in St. Louis and Kansas City, he was able to keep Ralph Street supplied with funds to keep the Osage River project going. But money got tight with Cravens because of foreclosures and in 1925, money therefore got equally tight with Street and his construction at the dam site. He was now unable to pay cash for the work there, and was incurring a mounting debt.

About the time Street was making his application to the State Public Service Commission in December, 1925, bank examiners appeared at the door of Cravens' oversized 12th floor, finely oak paneled land bank office. Alice B. Todd from her nearby office in the two-story, elaborate banking room, was among the first to greet the examiners. She was used to examiners in the bank, but these were different. These examiners were carrying guns.

MISS ALICE B. TODD

THE LADY BANKER

ALICE B. TODD would later recall the invasion of the armed bank examiners this way: "The advent of a group of examiners sent into the bank somewhere in December 1925, I recall they came in about noon time. It was an experience our bank had never had before because they were accompanied by Department of Justice men who were armed.

"This occurred during the afternoon. All of the files on the Land Bank were sealed during the afternoon. It was evidently apparently we were not going to be allowed to function during the examination. There were certain files located on the mezzanine floor which had to do with the trading and myself and a few of my associates—what we did was to go to that floor and remove from the files certain files which we were interested in in connection with the trading, and certain of Mr. Cravens' personal files, which were up there. The files connected with the trading were removed to the front mezzanine floor in which space the trading operations were being conducted, and those files were at all times there for the examiners, in our files. No files were removed which belonged to the bank. There were a good many times which we worked nearly all night."

She would also declare, "I had no interest in the Hydro-Power Company's books."

The incident occurred at the height of Alice B. Todd's remarkable rise in the banking world. Considering she was a high school dropout, no one would have predicted she would become one of the highest ranking female executives in Kansas City's business circle.

She was born in Salina, Kansas on February 4, 1885, the youngest of five children of Andrew G. Todd and Emaline V. Perrill Todd. The three older sisters, Gertrude, Adelaide, and Anna married and lived in Salina. A brother, Albert William also lived in Salina. Another brother, Harry Perrill moved to California. Alice Barbara was an attractive brunette. She attended Salina schools until after her sophomore year in high school when, because of her father's death in 1901, she found it necessary to provide for her own livelihood. After a short business course in stenography, she accepted a position with the H.D. Lee Mercantile Company in Salina. She spent five years there, then went with her mother to California where brother Harry resided. She was there nine years and was counted in the 1910 census as a resident of Los Angeles before returning to Salina in 1917 for a Christmas visit. During that visit Walter Cravens told her of his plan to start a joint stock land bank as provided for in the Federal Farm Loan Act of 1916 and invited her to join the new venture. Cravens himself, like Miss Todd, had worked for L. C. Staples of the H.D. Lee Mercantile Company before working for his father.

After securing her position with the mortgage company, she then joined Walter Cravens in January 1918, when he organized the Liberty Joint Stock Land Bank in Salina. She started at $75 ($915) per month as first assistant secretary, then in 1920 she was named secretary of the bank. Here, the relationship between Alice B. Todd and Walter Cravens developed into a very close and trusting one. Whether it was—outside of the affairs of business—purely a platonic relationship can only be surmised. Miss Todd appeared to be close with both Walter and his wife Bertha.

She, Cravens, her mother, her brother-in-law, the joint stock land bank and the Kansas City Finance Company used Miss Todd's bank account. In addition, she deposited in her account the funds of the Women's Chamber of Commerce of Kansas City for which she served as treasurer. When "some women at the bank became interested," in her account, she switched banks. Exactly how she kept track of the funds—how much belonged to whom—she was never able to explain.

She did the investing for members of her family and even for Cravens himself. She kept the records of the land bank and had the responsibility to make the reports to the Federal Farm Loan Board.

In 1922 when the bank moved from Salina to Kansas City, Miss Todd moved with it. And with Walter Cravens. She was promoted to secretary of the bank and her salary went to $200 ($2440) a month. The next year she received $300 per month and the next, $400 per month. In 1925 the bank's books showed she received $8965. She told later that she set her own salary. One year she had hospital care and Cravens paid for that out of bank funds.

Miss Todd devised the bank's record-keeping ledgers, she said, because the Farm Loan Board had not set up any standards for record keeping when the Farm Loan Act was passed. Cravens called the shots, Miss Todd signed the checks and Ralph Street spent the money when it came to matters of the Missouri Hydro Electric Power Company. Cravens was moving pretty fast, delving into automobile sales, farm mortgages, hydroelectric dams, safe deposits, finance companies, stocks and bonds, even managing farms that had been foreclosed on. Miss Todd—at least as she testified—tried to keep it all straight for him, trying to keep it all legal. And did until the armed bank examiners walked into the bank and took over.

Of the March 10, 1925 agreement between the joint stock land bank and the Missouri Hydro Electric Power Company pertaining to the trading of foreclosed mortgages for land in the flood area of the dam and selling them to the hydro company, Miss Todd insisted she had advised Cravens that he should obtain permission from the Federal Farm Loan Board for such action. Although, that permission was not requested, Cravens continued the practice and Miss Todd executed the agreements.

On the night of April 24, 1927, a group of government examiners walked into the bank, asked—whom Attorney Henry Conrad called a "scrubwoman,"—to open a room and the government began seizing records and sealing them. Alice B. Todd said about that night, "I was there not very much later. I recall it was ten or eleven o'clock at night when I was advised this entrance had been made."

Ten days later the bank was taken over by a receiver. Miss Todd said, "I have had no contact with the receiver at all. I was instructed when I first began this work that I was not to enter the bank floor and I haven't ."

She knew, of course, that Walter Cravens' empire was coming unraveled. And Alice B. Todd had tied her fate to his.

DAM BUILDERS MEET THE PEOPLE

WHILE ARMED BANK examiners roamed the aisles of the Kansas City Joint Stock Land Bank questioning Alice B. Todd, Ralph Street trolled the banking houses of New York City searching for a backer for his dream. And the people whose lives would be disrupted by the building of a monstrous dam on the Osage River were being offered an opportunity to express their opinion about that dam.

The Federal Power Commission controlled the construction of generating plants on navigable rivers in the country, but Missouri's Public Service Commission decided if such a plant was necessary for state residents and was it convenient for the public to have it built. The December, 1925 hearing was called to allow the Missouri Hydro-Electric Company to present their case that a dam and generating plant on the Osage River was not only necessary, but it would be convenient to the residents to have the structure.

On that 23rd of December, Public Service Commission Case Number 4632 was ready to be heard. Henry S. Conrad, a Kansas City attorney, appeared for the Company while C.O.Calkin, prosecuting attorney and Leonard Franklin, presiding judge of Camden County, F.M. Brady, prosecuting attorney and Presiding Judge Henry Lay from Benton County and Prosecuting Attorney Sam Haley of Cole County were listed in the hearing transcript as appearing for the opposition.

Donald Fitch, who had been an assistant to Ralph Street since 1922, was the first to testify to the commission. Summing up his description of the Osage River Project for the commission, Fitch said the project plans as drawn up by the Charles P. Hawley Engineering Company of Washington and as surveyed and mapped by Burns and McDonnell had been reviewed by the Army engineers for the Federal Power Commission, by Dr. Buehler, state geologist, and by Professor Riggs of the University of Michigan representing the investment bankers and all of them had approved the feasibility of the project. He told the commission of an agreement with the state highway department to provide a roadway atop the dam structure, thus creating a bridge across the Osage, of the developments the company built at the site of the dam and that the company had so far expended $1,850,000 on the property.

In regards to the fishing in the Osage, Fitch said that fishing below the dam would not be disturbed and that above the dam, new fish hatcheries would provide, "As many fish, if not more, than have been there previously."

"An item which we have not considered to date," Fitch said, vastly underestimating the future, "is the resort feature. We firmly believe that a lake of this size and depth situated within easy driving distance of Kansas City and St. Louis and located on good roads as this will be, we believe that a great number of people will be attracted there to enjoy just the pleasure facilities of the project."

He was not as prescient about the future of coal however. "Geologists estimate that the end of the coal supply (needed to furnish energy to steam-powered generating plants) is in sight," he told the commission, making a case for waterpower.

Sam Haley asked Fitch about the plans the company had for replacing the Camden County seat at Linn Creek after the dam flooded the town of 400 residents under forty feet of water.

"We have offered to build the county a new court house," Fitch said. "Even going so far as having the firm of Keene and Simpson draw up a plan of a court house to cost $60,000 and to build it, wherever the county wishes it."

But, he admitted, the offer had not been put in writing nor had it been made to the county court in session.

In the matter of taxes after the company took over thousands of acres in Camden County which Haley termed, "Simply meanderings of the Osage River," Fitch said it was customary to pro rate the value of the project among the four affected counties. To which Judge Lay of Benton County asked, "You are not a lawyer, Mr. Fitch?"

"No sir."

"Well, your supposition would be of very little force."

When Haley asked about the cemeteries that would be inundated, Fitch could name only two. Asked about their intention of, "strangling the town of Linn Creek and reducing the price of the property," Fitch replied, "We have paid most liberally for all of the property we have acquired in Linn Creek," but, then admitted some of the property had been acquired by trade.

Fitch said the Osage Project would furnish electrical power cheaper than anywhere in the state. The cheapest power production he knew about in the state was from two plants using pulverized coal-driven steam operations in East St. Louis and Kansas City Power and Light's northeast plant that had generating costs of around three-fourths of a cent per kilowatt-hour versus the six and a half mill costs planned by the Missouri Hydro-Electric Company. "Two men can run this station," he said. "There is no fuel."

The City of St. Louis had informed Missouri Hydro-Electric, Fitch said, that by 1930 they would be interested in, "joining transmission lines with us for the purpose of transmitting power back and forth."

Kansas City Power and Light Company said that by, "1928 they would be in position to use our entire power output if we chose to sell it all to them which we prefer not to do."

"It is the interior of the state we would prefer to serve," Fitch said. "It will save us transmission line losses. The savings that this project would effect are far greater in the central part of the state where rates are high than they would be in Kansas City or St Louis."

Fitch agreed that he thought fifty percent of the flooded area would be in Camden County and would divide it into two parts from east to west.

When Sam Haley asked Fitch if he knew that it would take a two thirds majority of the qualified voters to move the county seat from Linn Creek and what plans had been made to take care of it, Fitch said he was aware of the requirements to move the county seat and that no arrangements had been made to take care of that detail. Attorney Conrad for the Company then told the Commission that the company's contention is that, "we have the power and authority of eminent domain under the Federal Act, if that becomes necessary, but that is not our policy. It is to the contrary, but the ultimate source of authority we think is there."

Judge Lay of Benton County prefaced his questioning of Fitch and B.S. Philbrick, an engineer from the Hawley Company, with, "I do not appear here in any degree of opposing the proposition," and directed the majority of his questions to the subject of taxes, county roads and bridges and low and high water conditions in Warsaw as a result of the dam. He did engage Fitch on the claim about the amount of money that would be spent in the four counties.

> JUDGE LAY: Now, you did say twelve million dollars would be expended?
> MR. FITCH: Around twelve million. Of course that doesn't include the whole project. That is just what will be spent there for labor and things of that kind.
> JUDGE LAY: Well, that will substantially all be spent in Miller County?
> MR. FITCH: The greater end of it will be spent in the site of the dam.

Philbrick, who had worldwide experience designing and building power plants, in answering Conrad's question about success of building such plants, said, "There hasn't been a single failure along these lines in the United States. I know of failures in foreign countries, that is from a financial standpoint on account of it being a promoting scheme where they did not have the safeguards they have here in this country."

He may have spoken too soon about safeguards against schemes.

To open the phase of testimony from citizens, Robert J. Harvey of Eldon provided some of the more colorful and interesting language. Harvey identified himself as Miller County's largest taxpayer and was addressed by all of his questioners as "Colonel."

"By getting this power there," he said about the benefits to the town of Eldon, "we expect to put in some factories there and employ this labor and keep it at home."

He said Eldon was paying the highest price for power and that was retarding it from getting shoe factories. Describing a paint factory in town, he said, "they are working principally women and it doesn't do the town very much good from the financial standpoint. They are not building any houses nor paying any taxes."

"A man can," he said, "if he lives out in the Ozarks, bring the whole family to town and work himself and his wife, if not too old, and his boys and his girls and those that would be younger and want to go to school, we have a good school for them."

As to the fate of Camden County, he said the people there could come over to Miller County. "We'd be glad to have them." He said Camden County needed to get a better class of farmers. "Put some Germans in there, some men that will farm scientifically and they will raise more."

"I believe the Master understood what he was doing when he made this Osage River and I believe that it was made for the purpose of when the (railroad) ties was all brought in, to put it to some better and more useful purpose."

Harvey thought, "The lay of the country is just adapted to boating."

He said, "We see we are going to have a city there (Eldon)."

When asked what would bring the city to Eldon, he replied, "Why, it will be the cheaper power for our machinery and shoe factories. We will have this Public Service Commission straighten them out if they don't come down (in price). We will just straighten them out is what we will do. It is going to be the uplift of the state."

J.H. Savage of Warsaw followed Harvey. Conrad asked what Savage thought of the project. "I am one of the natives," he said, "and we have too many natives. We want new blood and I figure it will bring them in and as a result we will have diversified farming, cheaper power, better roads and our taxes will be reduced."

W.A. Duell of Versailles, president of the First National Bank there and the president of the Chamber of Commerce said he had not heard of any opposition to the project and he thought it would help Versailles get new industry.

A.M. Pope of Linn Creek told Conrad there were, "eight or ten, maybe more," stores in Linn Creek. He said there was no electrical power in Linn Creek at the present time. Judge Lay asked Pope about taxes in Linn Creek. "It has been reported to the people down there that they will get their pro rata share of the taxes of the whole project, hasn't it?"

> MR. POPE: I think they claim that we would get as much tax out of the dam proposition if they go ahead and build it as we are getting now, possibly more, I believe is the way they state it."
>
> JUDGE LAY: That comes entirely from those representing the dam. You haven't got that from the legal advisers of your county?
>
> MR. POPE: I think I heard Mr. Cravens say that.

Leonard Franklin, presiding judge of the Camden County Court said he didn't think there was any big objection to the dam in Camden County. Sam Haley asked him if any representations had been made to the county court as to what arrangements, if any, will be made with reference to a county seat or courthouse. "Not that I know of," he replied.

"As I understand," Haley said, "as presiding judge of the

county court of Camden County, you are not antagonistic to the proposition but want to conserve the interests of your people there with reference to the taking care of roads and bridges and a court house?"

"Yes, sir," Franklin answered. "That is the reason I appeared."

Franklin told the commission that in 1924 the assessed valuation of Camden County was something over five million dollars.

W.G. Nelson, county clerk of Camden County, said the county tax charges ran around $90,000 total, but some of the funds were behind. The average assessed value of farmland in the county was $7.98 per acre. He thought that the dam project would bring in more tax money than the county had ever had because of new industry and the county's share of taxable valuation of the project.

Sam Haley asked, "You figure if you build a new county seat then you will be in position to compete with Warsaw, Versailles and Eldon for these flourishing enterprises?"

"I certainly do," Nelson said.

"And, in addition thereto, you will get electric energy at cheap rates?"

"I certainly do," Nelson answered again. "We have never had any."

Sam Haley again, "You are employed and have been for some eight months by the dam people?"

"Yes, sir," Nelson admitted.

Joe Foster, acting vice president of Camden County Bank in Linn Creek told the commission that the people of Linn Creek would like to have a, "Fair and square understanding with the promoters of the project about what they are to get for their property and have that proposition guaranteed." Further, he said, "If there is a proposition submitted to remove the county seat out of the way, that the property owners of Linn Creek would be compelled to fight it teeth and toenails because they couldn't be expected to vote the county seat right out from under their noses and away from their banks and their stores and their businesses until they have had an absolute agreement about the price. If that was done, I don't see any reason then why they couldn't cooperate."

After Foster's testimony, the hearing concluded. The people of the Missouri Hydro-Electric Power Company must have breathed a huge sigh of relief. The anticipated opposition to their dam on the Osage River that would flood the town of Linn Creek, divide Camden County in half and threaten the town of Warsaw with floods and mud flats had not materialized. The level of opposition had been centered on taxes, roads and bridges, lake levels and a new courthouse for Camden County. All manageable items.

But, only one shoe had been dropped. Shoes come in pairs. And some own more than one pair.

INDICTED

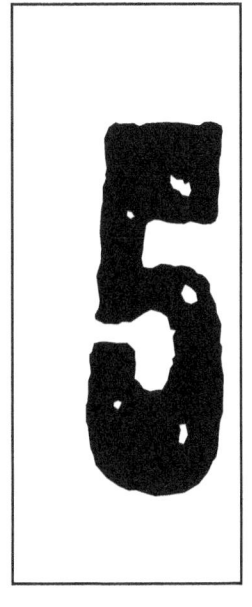

AS THE NEW YEAR, 1926, started, Street, Cravens and the rest of the Hydro-Electric company awaited the decision of the Missouri Public Service Commission while watching nervously, the squad of examiners who came into the Kansas City Joint-Stock Land Bank carrying guns and going up and down the bank aisles opening drawers and looking on all the shelves.

Sharp pencils and pens were standard equipment for bank examiners, but guns? Acting on complaints from bond and stockholders, the Justice Department was concerned enough about suspected irregularities to send an army of federal bank examiners into the Kansas City Joint Stock Land Bank reinforced by members of the Secret Service. They were the ones with the guns. They had been commissioned as examiners and were there accompanied by other agents of the government holding commissions as bank examiners. The crew would be in the land bank for the next 12 months going through ledgers, bank records, checks, etc. Certain books, papers and records of the bank would disappear and later reappear in the files of the Treasury Department in Washington, D.C.

On January 12, 1926, the Public Service Commission issued an order in response to the company's application. "In general," the order read, "the residents of the counties affected by this proposed project appear favorable to the project, except in Camden County where it appears that about one-half of the population of said county is opposed to the project."

The order stated that the applicant (Missouri Hydro-Electric Power Company) claimed to have offered to build a new courthouse and other buildings for the county, although, the applicant admitted that it had never presented that offer to the county court in session.

"While the counties are friendly to the project," the order stated, "they seek reasonable protection along three lines." Those lines concerned the question of public roads and bridges, the question of taxation and assurance of maintaining the level of the resulting lake.

"It therefore appears that the public interests will be best served," the commission wrote, "by requiring the applicant to secure the consent of the county courts."

This wasn't the decision the Missouri Hydro-Electric Company was hoping for. Camden and Benton Counties stood in the path of gaining a complete certificate from the commission.

On January 16, 1926, the presiding judge of the Morgan County Court, John A. Klein, wrote to the commission on stationary of the City Hotel in Versailles that the Morgan County Court consented to granting the certificate to the Missouri Hydro-Electric Company.

On January 18, 1926, the presiding judge, Lewis Chrismon, of the Miller County Court sent their letter of consent to the commission.

On that same day the Camden County Court met informally in a meeting that did not have the minutes recorded in the official records of the county, but was described by Camden County Sheriff S.C. Paxton to writer Louis LaCoss in the January 21 issue of the St. Louis *Globe-Democrat*, telling of the "unofficial meeting" with unnamed representatives of the Missouri Hydro-Electric Company. Judge W.F. Claiborne of Decatureville, in the sheriff's words, "riz right up and said he was against the dam and said he wasn't going to vote for it." Tom Edwards of Macks Creek said his district favored it, but Presiding Judge Leonard Franklin said he wasn't going to take sides for it or against it. He told the company representatives that since it took them more than 20 days to get a decision out of Jefferson City on the Certificate of Public Convenience and Necessity, "I'll be dadburned if you're agoin' to come down here and get us to make a decision in half a day."

Camden County Clerk W.G. Nelson summed up the meeting in a letter to the commission saying that Claiborne opposed the certificate, Edwards representing the first district of the county which contains the entire amount of land to be inundated favored it but that Presiding Judge Leonard Franklin refused to make any decision, indicating he might decide by the February meeting.

In a letter to the commission, L.D. Duff of Jackson County, Missouri, in support of the Missouri Hydro-Electric Company, told of his interview of the Camden County Court judges and citizens of the county on January 18. Duff said he explained to Judge Claiborne of Decatureville that the State Tax Commission would assess the whole project and the amount of taxes would be distributed among the four counties. Claiborne told Duff that talk was cheap and that people in his district opposed the project. Duff confirmed that Judge Edwards favored the project and that Judge Franklin refused to commit himself.

Duff wrote that on the next day, January 19, he and four other representatives of the Missouri Hydro-Electric Company prepared petitions to the Public Service Commission requesting that the certificate be granted. He sent to the commission 25 pages containing 503 signatures of Camden County property owners in favor of the project. Among them were the names of Collector W.O. Esther, Deputy Collector W.C. Jeffries, Postmaster John McCrory and County Clerk W.G. Nelson.

Duff further wrote that Judge Claiborne's district was in the southern part of the county and would not be affected by the project. Duff said he and the others representing the company interviewed 190 citizens of Judge Claiborne's district and only eight declined to sign the petition. He wrote that, "Practically all of Judge Claiborne's family signed the petition and that nearly all of the property owners of Linn Creek signed the petition." He declared that the sentiment of the people of Camden County was overwhelmingly in favor or the project.

Sheriff Paxton, however, told La Coss and the *Globe-Democrat* that he thought the sentiment in Linn Creek was about "Half and half."

"Them as hasn't got much invested here and see a good trade in sight are willing to get out from under and let the old town sink. But them as has their homes and business and has lived here all their lives and have their relatives buried up on the hill are not so ready to get out."

Judge Tom Edwards wrote his own letter to the Public Service Commission. He said that the Missouri Hydro-Electric Company had offered the county every fair and equitable term that was possible. "I sincerely hope that you will grant them the permit," he wrote.

The former judge from the county's first district, R.J. Brown wrote the commission on January 19 that he earnestly hoped that the certificate would be granted. "I was present at the hearing before our county court and this company made every fair and reasonable offer that was possible for them to do and I feel that the court should have granted them the consent asked for."

Brown said that, "A large majority of the people in the first district," was in favor of the project and that they should be taken into consideration far more than the rest of the county because the first district was the one most affected by the project.

Benton County gave their approval for the certificate on January 21, but with a stipulation containing points on replacement of roads and bridges, water level of the lake and tax assessment.

The Hydro-Electric Company then made a motion by letter to the commission asking that the January 12 Order be modified to grant the certificate asked for as the counties had all given their consent required by the order except for Camden County in which one of the judges of the county court had given his consent and as his district was the one most affected, that should constitute consent.

The Company followed that motion with another on January 22 asking for a rehearing on their request for a certificate of Public Convenience and Necessity. The commission erred, the motion said, in their order of January 12 which made the granting of the certificate dependent on the applicant's ability to negotiate a contract with the four counties. The motion termed the commission's actions "*ultra vires*," meaning beyond the power and scope of the commission. It was the commission's duty to grant the certificate, the company maintained, and it could not be delegated to the counties. The countys; rights and the relief necessary and incident are irrelevant to the granting of the certificate as they are protected by the courts. The commission had already, in the January 12 order, determined that a public convenience and necessity existed for the contemplated improvements as set forth in the application.

The commission responded by scheduling another public hearing for January 26. Following that hearing, the commission issued a new order granting the Certificate of Public Convenience and Necessity to the Missouri Hydro-Electric Company with the following stipulations therein: For Benton County, the Company agreed to replace all roads and bridges rendered useless by the construction of the dam and that in case of controversy, the Public Service Commission would have jurisdiction to decide; the water level of the lake shall be maintained as nearly as possible at constant level and all swamps and mudflats shall be remedied; and the company shall use best efforts to secure passage of a law providing for pro-rating of the assessed valuation among counties affected by the dam to be similar to the assessment of railroads.

The order stated that the company and the County Court of Camden County agreed that for and in consideration of the County Court giving its consent of issuing the certificate, the same stipulations made to Benton County would be in effect in addition to the commitment by the company to reimburse the county $60,000 to build a new courthouse and jail.

The Camden County Court, however, did not, in fact, agree to any such thing. What did happen was that following the January 26, 1926 hearing, Presiding Judge Leonard Franklin signed a contract with the Missouri Hydro-Electric Company while on a visit to Jefferson City and the capitol building. When Associate Judge Claiborne heard about it, he was upset and wrote a letter to the Commission protesting the contract.

Other problems surfaced for Ralph Street and his dream.

"My heart was in this project and I put forth the very best efforts I could," he told the Public Service Commission during a later session.

Street told how he stopped all activity at the dam site in December 1925, then filed the application for the certificate for Convenience and Necessity. The government had started an investigation of Guy Huston and that investigation lead them to Walter Cravens and the Kansas City Joint Stock Land Bank. That day in December 1925, when the gun-toting bank examiners walked in, changed the whole course of events. Walter Cravens and his Kansas City Joint Stock Land Bank became the subject of government investigation as well as Guy Huston.

Street put it this way, "After the Land Bank investigation started with Mr. Cravens (December 1925)—he was responsible for bringing Mr. Huston into the picture—(Mr. Cravens) ceased to be active."

Street had spent Christmas 1925 in Chicago for an interview with a Mr. Denman, vice president and general manager of the United Power & Light Company, the holding company for Kansas City Power & Light Company. He also met with the manager of the Kansas City Railway and gave them an option in January 1926 for the controlling interest in the dam. That option was not exercised. Street went back to New York on January 30, 1926 to meet with representatives of American Brown-Boverie.

"I spent about three weeks with the engineers of that department and they made a favorable report to the president, Mr. Weiler. I met Mr. Weiler for the first time about eleven o'clock on Saturday morning and he had before him the report which the engineering department had made on the project. I remember he sent out and had some sandwiches and milk sent in and we continued the conference until about three o'clock in the afternoon. He said, 'You are a lawyer, and I have asked my lawyer to remain down this afternoon in hopes that you could get together. I will call him up and you go over there and get up the necessary papers and bring them back to me Monday morning and I will let you have the money.'"

It didn't happen that way. Street saw the lawyer who said the company was organized for manufacturing and had no authority to make a loan to secure business. He told Street that if they made the loan over his protest he would resign.

"Three more weeks gone," was how Street put it.

Next he went to Westinghouse. "I went through the same proceedings there," he said. "At the end of three weeks the executive engineer in the New York office took me over there and said we are going into the project with you, and the next day I had arranged to see Mr. Hare, the president, but he turned it down. Something had changed the situation from one day to the next."

Street went to Peabody, Houghteling and Company who employed Ford, Bacon and Davis to investigate the project. Ford, Bacon and Davis made a favorable report, but Peabody, Houghteling and Company chose not to go into the project without a contract to sell the power generated at the dam.

"We took it up to Harrimans," Street told it, "but it was the same situation. I became convinced we could not do anything without a power contract."

Back in Linn Creek, J. W. Vincent, in the *Reveille*, expressed concerns about relocating the county seat.

"In order for a vote to be taken on the proposition (to move the county seat), one-fourth of the voters of the county must present a petition to that effect. Then, for it to carry, a two-thirds majority must be obtained. I'm not so sure that such a majority will vote for the project."

Vincent listed the jealousy and competition among the other towns in the county vying for the $60,000 pledged by the company to build a new courthouse as reasons he doubted passage of the vote. If the vote failed, it would be another four years before such a vote could be taken again.

At the April 10 meeting of the Camden County Court they finally would give or withhold their consent of the certificate. The company pledged to pay the county for public buildings submerged or damaged which included $60,000 for the courthouse and tract of land in Linn Creek. The company would build or replace roads, bridges and crossings damaged, submerged or rendered impassable by the lake waters. Third, the water level of the lake after construction would as nearly as possible be maintained at a constant level, swamps and mudflats would be drained and treated with oil to prevent mosquitoes and other unhealthy conditions. Fourth, the company would use their best efforts to secure passage of a law providing for pro-rating of assessed valuations similar to assessment of railroads.

The contract, signed by Walter Cravens and Walter Essyell for the Missouri Hydro-Electric Power Company was entered into the Camden County Court records as approved.

Street hadn't slowed his efforts to get the dam built. He talked with who he called the "street railways," (the trolley system) then back to United Power & Light Company who were reluctant to go with the Hydro-Electric Company unless they could give assurance of turning out the quantity of power claimed and that the reservoir could hold the water and power could be generated as cheaply as Street said it could. The proposal was first discussed in a meeting at Pittsburg, then again days later in New York. The committee was concerned that the Bagnell dam would not be completed at a cost that would enable the sale of electrical power as cheaply as was being produced at a new coal-fired plant northeast of Kansas City.

"We spent all summer with the engineers," Street said, "and by July 21 we had a tentative agreement with Mr. Denman and Mr. Porter for a power contract. I was invited to go back to Chicago and meet with the board of directors where the contract would be ratified. That board of director's meeting continued to a second meeting, then a third and I finally became satisfied that they were not sincere."

Street's tenacity drove him on. He was working for, what to him must have seemed like a paltry sum, $800 per month into a drawing fund. He went to Harris and Forbes in New York and to John Nickerson. Both turned him down because he could not show them a power contract.

In late October or early November 1926, Street had begun talks with Dillon, Read and Company. In December they invited Stone & Webster Engineering Company to participate. Stone & Webster had an impressive record in designing and building hydroelectric plants all over the world. Street met with Mr. Snyder of Stone & Webster and Mr. Waddell of Dillon, Read and company. Shortly before Christmas, 1926, the two men told Street they would go back to report to their partners and if the partners saw the project as they did, Street would be invited back to talk with them. Street did not have to go traveling that Christmas, but left immediately after to continue negotiations. By January 7, 1927, those negotiations broke down and Street was out searching for a backer again.

On the fourth of November 1926, the Public Service Commission had complied with a subpoena from the Western District Federal Court for all the papers in its possession pertaining to the request and the issuance of a certificate of Public Convenience and Necessity to the Missouri Hydro-Electric Company.

In April 1927, the Kansas City *Times* reported that the United Light and Power Company had not agreed to terms with the Hydro-Electric Company to furnish power to Kansas City Power and Light.

"That negative action," said the *Times*, "while it may not close the door to continued negotiations of new proposals, will permit the local promoters of the Bagnell Project to submit their plan to other possible current buyers, including St. Louis power interests."

The Kansas City *Journal-Post* wrote that, "Failure of the parent company controlling the Kansas City Power and Light Company to accept the Osage dam power project, is viewed to financial circles here as a severe blow to the hydroelectric scheme."

Chester C. Smith, vice president and secretary of Kansas City Power and Light Company told the *Journal-Post* that officials of the holding company feared that if the project was not completed within the cost and time limits, it would not be a success.

The failure to land a contract with the Kansas City firm dealt a severe blow to Street's dream. He summed up his work on the Bagnell project this way: "When we started in on this project, it only took a part of the time, but as the matter progressed I spent the greater part of two years in New York and what was once a fairly lucrative income ceased to exist from my law practice and the only income I had was the small drawing account my associates agreed that I should have. Since the summer of 1925 I have devoted practically all my time to it."

He said, "I was offered a partnership in two or three concerns. I was somewhat flattered."

He tried Spencer Trask and The Foundation Company and spent his time until April trying to work out a deal with them, but, again, the lack of a power contract nixed the deal.

"About that time, Mr. Waddell (Dillon, Read and Company) called me and said he understood we were not making any progress and he wanted us to come back and talk it over further and said, 'The door will still be open.'"

By the end of April they had worked out an option contract. If Dillon, Read and Company picked up the option, it would be the only good news the Hydro-Electric Company was to receive in 1927.

A grand jury had been convened at the federal court in Kansas City, Kansas, and out of that came a blow that threatened to be lethal to the Missouri Hydro-Electric Company. On April 23, 1927, Federal Judge John C. Pollock returned indictments against seven individuals and one corporation connected with the company. Among those indicted were Walter Cravens and Ralph Street and five other officers in the Kansas City Joint Stock Land Bank along with the Cravens Mortgage Company of Salina, Kansas.

Four companies headed by Walter Cravens benefitted from misuse of land bank funds, government investigators alleged. The companies were, Kansas City Finance Company, Missouri Kansas Farms Company, Cravens Mortgage Company, Salina, Kansas, and the Missouri Hydro-Electric Power Company. The government's contention was that bank funds were "lent" to the private companies on "straw" mortgages without genuine security. Records of the Missouri Public Service Commission revealed that $1,227,000 ($14,908,050) was invested in the Missouri Hydro-Electric Power Company in the acquisition of 30,000 acres of land.

The Linn Creek *Reveille* reported that on April 22, 1927, the recorder of deeds for Camden County recorded fifteen deeds from the Farmer's Fund, Incorporated, conveying about 6470 acres of land to various parties for the sum of $1 and other valuable considerations, accompanied by fifteen mortgages in the aggregate sum of $239,000

($2,903,850). On the following Monday, fifteen more deeds were recorded conveying the same lands back to Land Fund Incorporated, also for $1 and other valuable considerations. The various liens averaged $37 per acre.

The charges in the Kansas indictments were, among others, fraud, mainly involving the use of the mail. Judge Pollock, at the suggestion of U.S. District Attorney Al F. Williams, set bond for the seven men and the corporation at $10,000 each.

What the government said the indicted seven were doing was writing checks on the Land Bank and laundering the money through the Kansas City Finance Company, a corporation created by Walter Cravens, and on to the Cravens Mortgage Company as commissions on all the farm mortgages in Kansas and Missouri whether the Mortgage Company had actually negotiated the loans or not. The practice netted the mortgage company $537,283 in commissions between 1918 and 1926. The government called the transactions fraud that deprived the stockholders of the Land Bank of money earned.

The sales commission agreement between the mortgage company and the Land Bank had started with a verbal agreement when the Land Bank was first formed in Salina in 1917. The indictment did not charge that the mortgage company was not entitled to any commission, but left it to the bookkeepers and auditors to sort out.

Two days later, a grand jury was convened across the state line in Kansas City, Missouri. A dispatch to the New York *Journal of Commerce* stated:

> "For the second time within six days officials of Kansas City Joint Stock Land Bank were indicted by the Federal Grand Jury. The hydroelectric promotion of Walter Cravens' group at Bagnell, Mo. was the basis of today's grand jury indictments."

The indictments, containing 50 counts, alleged that false entries were made in the books of the land bank, there was a conspiracy to defraud stockholders of the land bank; there was manipulation in loans and money between the land bank, the Missouri Hydro-Electric Company, the Farmers Fund Company and the Kansas City Finance Company.

That afternoon's indictment explained the Government's allegation that Walter Cravens and his associates were in a huge conspiracy to finance the preliminary construction work on a huge hydroelectric project at Bagnell, Missouri

Stripped of legal verbiage, the indictments accused land bank officials of embezzlement of one million dollars of bank funds which were used, it was alleged, in financing the power project.

Government officials there said that, 'the surface has only been scratched' and indicated that the grand jury would continue to probe into the affairs of the land bank for several months.

After two days investigation, forty-five specific cases of falsifying mortgage records of the land bank were uncovered according to the indictment. It was alleged that, "forty-five mortgages . . . totaling $707,000 were signed by boys under twenty-one years of age, by improvident Negroes and by destitute persons who never had anything given as security."

The borrowers, the government charged were, "merely employed to sign notes to cover money taken from the bank to finance the Ozark Bagnell, Missouri Dam project."

The Springfield, Missouri *News* related that one of the indictments charged that Walter Johnson, a Sedalia Negro was approached by an agent of the Missouri Hydro-Electric Power Company on August 1, 1926, and asked to sign a note and mortgage for $30,000 made out to the Kansas City Joint Stock Land Bank.

Five of the land bank officers indicted in Kansas City, Kansas, made bond for $10,000 on April 28. The five, all from Salina, Kansas, were the three Cravens, J. B. Smith and Thomas Comerford. Walter Cravens and Ralph Street were reported to be on their way back from the East Coast where, on April 27, Ralph Street signed a contract with Stone & Webster and the holding company Dillon, Read and Company to finance the dam.

The grand jury indictments in Missouri were more sweeping than the ones that had come from the Federal Court in Kansas. Individuals indicted along with the four Cravens and Ralph Street were Miss Alice B. Todd, secretary of the Land Bank and one of only two female executives in joint stock land banks in the nation, W. D.

O'Bannon, attorney of Sedalia, Missouri, and Guy Huston. Companies indicted were the Guy Houston & Company in Chicago and the Guy Huston & Company in New York, the Missouri Hydro-Electric Company, Cravens Mortgage Company, Missouri-Kansas Farms Company, the Kansas City Finance Company, the Kansas City Joint Stock Land Bank, and the O'Bannon and Share Attorneys of Sedalia, Missouri.

Two practices were outlined in the indictments. One practice was the commission arrangement with the Cravens' Mortgage Company on all loans made in Kansas since 1918 whether the loans were negotiated by the mortgage company's agents or other agencies. The second practice alleged that the mortgage company drew sight drafts on the Kansas City Finance Company, a corporation formed by Walter Cravens, to obtain cash to redeem maturing bonds and guaranty certificates which were obligations of the mortgage company and that Walter Cravens drew checks on the Land Bank in favor of the finance company to honor the drafts and that false entries in the Land Bank's books were resorted to to conceal the issuance of the checks.

The government said those checks from the Land Bank to the mortgage company were a fraud upon the Land Bank and its stockholders and became a loss sustained by the Land Bank and its stockholders.

Those indicted by the Missouri Grand Jury made bond on May 10 according to the Kansas City *Journal-Post*. Walter Cravens was the first to be released on bonds secured by F.W. Zwanzig, sheriff of Morgan County Missouri, and E. H. Cravens, mayor of Excelsior Springs. Mrs. L. G. Hill of Excelsior Springs, made the surety bond for Walter Cravens' father, Richard Price Cravens. Mrs. Hill offered real estate valued at $100,000 ($1,215,000). Six bondsmen qualified for a total of $143,000 for the bond of R. H. Cravens. They included L. C. Gray, manager of the Southwestern Millers Mutual Insurance Company and others, all from Versailles including Mayor Egdorf. J. B. Billingham of Platte City, Harry Hale of Warrensburg and W. D. O'Bannon, a Sedalia attorney, signed the bond for Alice B. Todd.

On May 4, 1927, Walter Cravens and Alice B. Todd cleaned out their desks and left the Kansas City Joint Stock Land Bank forever. The Bank had defaulted on its obligations and the Federal Farm Loan Board, in accordance with the terms of the Federal Farm Loan Act, declared the bank to be insolvent. William R. Compton, a St. Louis Investment broker, was appointed receiver of the Kansas City Joint-Stock Land Bank. Compton took charge of the bank's assets, records and books. Walter Cravens' offer to assist the receiver was not accepted. Alice B. Todd was told not to contact the receiver.

DREAM TURNS TO NIGHTMARE, wrote Jack D. Craig of the Kansas City *Journal-Post* on May 25, 1927.

"With all faith in the promotion of the Osage River hydroelectric project destroyed by the recent troubles of the promoters, the dream of Walter Cravens, Ralph Street and their associates, the promotion has become a nightmare to Linn Creek and Camden County."

"No one here believes the project will ever succeed," Craig wrote from Linn Creek, "and the community finds itself faced with problems difficult to solve. It estimates it will cost the county $2,000,000 ($24,300,000) to get back to the place it occupied before the glib-tongued agents of the Farmers Fund, Inc, persuaded many of the best farmers to sell outright their holdings here and talked residents of Linn Creek into parting with the title to homesteads their grandfathers occupied.

"The exploitation to date has resulted in between 150 and 200 of the county's most influential farmers leaving the section for farms they acquired through the manipulation of the Cravens group. Their farms are lying idle or are being farmed by tenants."

Craig wrote of the loss in tax revenue by the county because of the movement of the farmers and the fact that the Farmers Fund had not paid any taxes at all.

The Horseshoe Bend school district was reported as shortening its school year to four months, but still having outstanding warrants of $450 due the teachers. School district number 11 ran only four months and was forced to close for lack of funds. The Linn Creek school was forced to borrow $500 to complete the school year. The Bagnell schools and the Pleasant Grove District were in difficulty financially and were encouraged by state officials to consolidate their independent school districts.

Estimates by June 1927, had the hydroelectric company acquiring half the properties in Linn Creek with the former owners occupying the properties as tenants. The landlords refused to repair the properties and the tenants were told if the roof leaks, fix it or let it leak.

When word of the indictments against the dam promoters reached Linn Creek, the Camden County Commissioners instructed tax collector Egel Farrish to file suit against delinquent taxpayers. Fifteen such suits were filed.

Craig completed his article with,

"Linn Creek did not want to become a lake bottom, but it felt it ought not hamper a state development. Now it is viewing itself as a loser. If the project should by any chance succeed, the town will be wiped out. If the project fails, as Linn Creek believes it will, it is faced with a reconstruction problem which would baffle a less sturdy people."

Things didn't get any better for Walter Cravens. On July 1, 1927, The Kansas City *Post* announced that a warrant had been issued for Cravens on charges in Toledo, Ohio. A Federal Grand Jury there on June 2, returned indictments against Cravens and seven others including Guy Huston and his brother John. The indictment alleged the defendants conspired to defraud stockholders and the public in connection with the operations of the Farmers Fund of Illinois, Inc., the Farms Company of Massachusetts and the Missouri-Kansas Farmers Company that Cravens had started. The companies, the indictment stated, were started, ostensibly to make loans to farmers from the sale of stock. Instead, the money was used to cover up losses in land banks and no loans were ever made to farmers.

WARRANT ISSUED FOR CRAVENS ON TOLEDO CHARGES

Arrest Asked After Copy of Indictment, Returned June 2, Is Received Here.

Bank examiners, postal inspectors and government agents

conferred in Missouri with special attorneys general regarding the next move in the investigation when the Kansas City Grand Jury reconvened in July.

At a federal court session in July, according to the *Journal-Post*, Henry Conrad sought to obtain a court order to force the government to return the papers and records they had removed from the Kansas City Joint Stock Land Bank during the 12-month investigation of bank files. Conrad maintained the records were necessary for bank business.

Forest W. Hanna, the attorney for the land bank, testified that on the night of April 24, 1927, he was contacted by Miss Todd and told that federal agents were investigating an unused part of the building and that she had ordered W. H. Davenport, secret service agent in charge of the Kansas City unit, and W. H. Tull, bank examiner to leave but that they refused to go. Tull told Conrad, during examination at the grand jury, that they refused to go because they had found evidence of a crime.

"Set forth one instance of a crime they found in those records," Conrad challenged Tull.

Tull recited a list of 100 notes made out to alleged "straw men" found in the records.

"Was there any other evidence of crime?" Conrad asked.

Tull looked at the government prosecutor who told him, "You may answer."

"There was evidence that some $466,000 ($5,661,900) was diverted from bank funds to the Missouri Hydro-Electric Power Company," Tull said.

"Do you mean that sum had been stolen from the bank?" Conrad asked, incredulously.

Tull said, "Yes, that's what I mean."

In August, the *Missouri Ruralist* magazine said, "Collapse of the Kansas City Joint Stock Land Bank, which was helping finance the big Bagnell power dam project has left Camden County in a bad way.

"All operations have stopped and no one can predict the outcome. It may be necessary for the state to help solve this problem."

The worst was yet to come for Cravens and Alice B. Todd. A 300-page indictment containing 88 counts was returned by the federal grand jury on August 4 against the two. The government had narrowed their target and had sent all the way from Washington, D.C. the assistant to the Attorney General of the United States to take the indictments to court and to prosecute the case.

TRIAL

GOVERNMENT INVESTIGATORS told the Kansas City *Journal* on August 5, 1927, the day after they testified in the third grand jury to delve into the affairs of the Kansas City Joint Stock Land Bank, that Walter Cravens' career as a financier and promoter would likely rival that of con men Charles Ponzi and C.C. Julian.

The 88 counts returned in the indictment were for false entries in the bank's books and misapplication of the bank's funds. Walter Cravens, as president of the bank was held responsible for all the counts. Alice. B. Todd's part in the transactions. the indictments claimed, was to so alter the bank's records that shortages of money would not show up on the bank's books. In one instance, Miss Todd was charged with paying a personal note to a Salina bank with money belonging to the land bank. Miss Todd's position as secretary of the bank made it possible for her to order entries and changes of accounts in the bank's records that kept knowledge of Cravens' activities from other employees of the bank, government agents said. They also claimed that in several instances entries concealing the alleged misappropria-

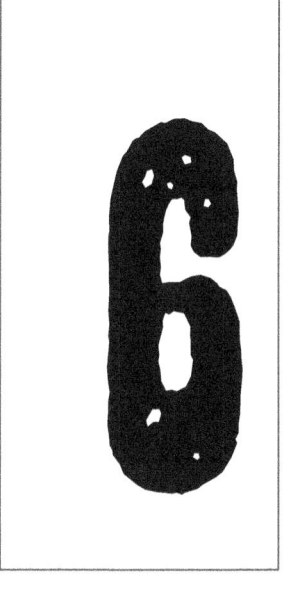

CRAVENS' 'PONZI' METHODS HINTED

Exploits in High Finance May Be Revealed in Land Bank Case.

56 DAM OVER TROUBLED WATERS

HEADLINE IN KANSAS CITY JOURNAL

tions of funds were found in Miss Todd's handwriting.

Cravens was charged in one count with paying out of land bank funds a $1000 attorney-fee contracted in a private suit against Guy Huston. The suit, as it turned out, was because Huston had reneged on his deal to shuffle funds into the hydroelectric project at Bagnell.

The government set a trial date for later in the year, but it would be spring in 1928 before the two would be tried.

Alice B. Todd was the only defendant to appear in court before Judge Merrill E. Otis on April 12, 1928, at a hearing on the previous April's grand jury indictment. The other defendants were represented by counsel.

The defense counsel entered a plea of abatement contending the indictments were found on evidence obtained by illegal methods. Roscoe Patterson and Nugent Dodds, representing the government, filed a demurrer, contending the plea did not state a good reason for having the indictments quashed.

The April 17, 1928 issue of the Linn Creek *Reveille* reported that the Bank of Bagnell had been closed by order of the board of directors. The State Finance Department took over. The bank ended 15 years of operation after the capital had been impaired by frozen loans.

That same month, Morgan Moulder, son of Fred J. Moulder, filed for Prosecuting Attorney of Camden County. He attended the Missouri State University and graduated from Cumberland University in Tennessee in 1927. He would be elected to the office the next November and become embroiled in the controversy between the Bagnell Dam Project and Camden County along with the town of Linn Creek.

Alice B. Todd's remarkable career as bookkeeper, accountant and finally ascending to secretary of the second largest Joint-Stock Land Bank in the country was entering a climax. Her lofty position ended when the receiver took over the bank. Now, her freedom was at risk. She and the man to whom she had tied her destiny, Walter Cravens, went on trial May 7, 1928, for misapplication of federal joint-stock land bank funds. Perhaps her thoughts ranged back to the day, with only two years in high school in tiny Salina, Kansas, when she accepted a job as a stenographer-bookkeeper at the H.D. Lee Mercantile Company in Salina in lieu of continuing her education. Or, perhaps, her thoughts were of her nine years spent in California and how she could have remained there and avoided this day.

But now, it was far more than likely it was trouble that was on her mind. That would include thoughts of the man himself, Walter Cravens. And exactly what her relationship with him had become. He was a handsome man with dark hair and good features and was a dynamo of an executive, always talking, even in modest terms, of great immodest feats to accomplish. Perhaps that was why, seven years ago when Cravens moved his whole land bank operation to Kansas City from Salina, she had made the move with him. Promises had been made; some of them kept, some not. She received a modest salary at the Cravens Mortgage Company ran by Walter's father ten years before, but in five years with Walter her salary had grown by almost ten times. Perhaps a small resentment was growing within. She had done all he had asked of her. Still, she had to have been an admirer of his intelligence, and possessed little doubt they would both be exonerated when he was given a chance to offer his explanation.

She was an attractive woman, and on court day, stylishly dressed, with the bearing expected of one of only two female executives in the country in federal land banks. Her thin lips were drawn in a straight line, a bit taut, until they intersected with the curvature of her cheeks. Her eyes were expressive with brows slightly raised, enough to show interest, but bordering on aloofness. Her dark hair was parted in the middle and was mid-length; too long for the "Bob," too short to be Victorian. The few in the courtroom were certain to have looked her over, especially the women.

The attendance in the courtroom was sparse, despite the fact the newspapers had called this one of the major trials in the history of the federal court in Kansas City. The core of the trial was farm mortgages, so it was a surprise somewhat that men and women, whose livelihood was tied to the Earth were so uncurious. Some would testify this day about mortgages they had and mortgages they had lost. Those people waited in the corridor, listening for their call. To the bookkeeper and accountant Alice B. Todd, the spectators and witnesses were numbers and entries in the bank's ledgers.

Representing Cravens and Alice B. Todd in court would be Henry S. Conrad, Kansas City attorney. Conrad had been the attorney for all of Cravens' enterprises and had been involved in federal and state hearings before farm loan boards, public service commissions and federal waterpower commissions. Conrad's legal reputation was as an attorney who saved bankers from legal morasses. Assisting Conrad would be R.R. Brewster, Forest W. Hanna and C.H. Kohler.

Nugent Dodds from Memphis, TN, the assistant attorney general to United States Attorney General John S. Sergeant, was the star of the prosecution team. He made the trip from Washington D.C. for this occasion. The defense team would note that in their addresses to the jury. Roscoe Patterson, U.S. district attorney, would be the chief prosecutor. Judge Sylvester Rush, special assistant to the U.S. attorney would assist. Cravens and Miss Todd were familiar with all of them as they had been in and out of the land bank offices since December 1925, when the investigation started.

From what Miss Todd had been told and what she had read in the newspapers, there would be as many as 200 witnesses to appear before the jury and Federal Judge Merrill E. Otis. She expected to be one of them.

Pre-court drama resulted when only twenty-three prospective jurors reported out of the 60 who had been called. Judge Otis determined there were not enough jurors to constitute a panel of twenty-eight rendered necessary by the provisions for peremptory challenges. The court ordered the U.S. Marshal to summon ten additional jurors from among the bystanders in the courthouse or in the immediate vicinity of the courthouse. When Conrad objected to what he called "packing," the jury by the government and stated that the jury was not a legal one, the marshal explained to the court how he had picked the extra ten jurors:

"I went into the place of business and went to the manager and told him I was going to take a man out of there for a juror, and I would let him pick the man if he wanted to, but I told him I wanted a man that looked to me like he would make a good juror, and if the man he picked didn't suit me, I would pick another."

The marshal said that in one instance he, "went to the assistant manager and told him I wanted to take a man for jury service, that he could designate a man that would disorganize the firm the least, and if he looked good I would take him, and if he didn't I would take another one, and the man he picked I didn't like so I picked another one."

When the jury was finally seated it contained eight members from the so-called "bystanders," the marshal had selected and four were from the regular panel of twenty-three. The defense objected again, complaining that one of the jurors had served in a previous panel that year.

In the pretrial questioning of the prospective jurors, Judge Otis asked them, "Is there any member of the panel who has formed or expressed an opinion concerning the merits of the case or the guilt or innocence of the defendants . . . ?"

Four panel members so expressed an opinion they held on the

innocence or guilt of the defendants and were excused. They were Fred Campbell, Mr. Sowers, F. Lockridge and A. Burrows. Two more jurors in addition to the four were excused from the panel for other reasons.

The Justice Department had selected this case based on the indictments returned by the August 4, 1927, Grand Jury against only Cravens and Miss Todd as the keystone case in the closing of the land bank. Although this grand jury had returned indictments of 88 counts against the two, two previous grand juries had indicted Cravens' father, two brothers, Ralph Street, Guy Huston, the Cravens Mortgage Company, the Missouri Hydro-Electric Power Company and others. Now it appeared that all of the Justice Department's eggs were in this one basket.

Nugent Dodds told the jury in his opening statement that the government would attempt to prove the two bank officials used several hundred thousand dollars of funds belonging to the Kansas City Joint Stock Land Bank to promote private enterprises and to cover up the transactions, they made false entries in the bank's books and in its reports to the federal farm loan board.

R.R. Brewster for the defense told the jury that if mistakes were made in the bank's books they were not made with the intent to defraud.

O.J. Field, chief of the bond division of the farm loan board, A.C. Williams, member of the board, and Mrs. Yula Harris, former bank employee were called to the witness stand to identify documents the prosecution would later use. Stanley C. Miller, the former assistant treasurer of the bank before it went into receivership, was among the prosecution's first witnesses. Patterson and his prosecution team began laying the groundwork for the 88 counts of misapplication of the bank's funds. A succession of voluminous journals and ledgers were brought forth along with records, receipts and cancelled checks and introduced to the court and to the jury to substantiate all 88 counts against the defendants. E.B. Fleming, a bookkeeper for the receiver, T.S Burgh, auditor for the First National Bank, Donald Fitch,

TRIAL 61

secretary/treasurer for the Missouri Hydro Electric Power Company and Miss Neva Hill, former bank employee were all marched to the witness chair to further identify documents for the prosecution. When the witnesses were cross examined by the defense attorneys, they were obligated to hold the large journals and ledgers on their laps as they traced the items in question from the original entry through the credit entries in several other manuals to its final disposition.

The monotony of the endless chain of financial ledger entries was broken somewhat by a lively argument between Nugent Dodds and Henry Conrad.

The magic pill that cured all ailments, Conrad contended, was a check for $497,000 from the Kansas City Finance Company to the bank in payment for farm lands the company had disposed of after the land bank had foreclosed on them.

Grand Jury testimony was introduced by the witnesses about, as one former bank employee named Maxwell put it, "The crooked practice of the defendants here (Cravens and Miss Todd) exercising continual and constant supervision over the bookkeeping of the bank. They ran it themselves."

That part of the Grand Jury testimony was reinforced by witnesses J.B. Smith and Thomas Comerford, bank directors, both of Salina, who told the Grand Jury that the meetings of the bank were faked and that the purported meetings they were supposed to have attended had never taken place and they never knew anything of them.

Judge Otis decided not to impound the jury. Eight of the jurors, all living in Kansas City, requested to be allowed to return to their homes at night. After conferring with attorneys on both sides, Judge Otis sent them home at night but cautioned them against discussing the trial with anyone.

The prosecution took up the first 33 counts of the indictment which they termed "misapplication counts." The money total of the first 33 counts was $133,922.61. This amount, the indictment said, was disbursed through the Kansas City Finance Company, a corporation controlled by the defendants, for the payment of expenses incurred on behalf of the Missouri Hydro-Electric Power Company, a corporation controlled by the defendant Cravens, and that it was charged on the books of the land bank as a "Special Bond Investment Account." The indictment charged that account did not show the real transactions.

S.C. Bennetts of Oakland, California, accountant of the Department of Justice who assisted Nugent Dodds in preparing the indictment, testified to the real transaction that took place in Count One of the first 33 counts. Count One concerned a check for $1,189.30.

> MR. PATTERSON: I hand you herewith Government's Exhibit 309 being letter heretofore introduced in evidence, from Miss Todd to you, and ask if that is the item of $1,189.30 -- if that is one of those items recited in that exhibit as having been disbursed to the Missouri Hydro-Electric Power Company for logging expenses?
> MR. BENNETTS: Exhibit 309 shows disbursement of that identical item as logging expense.
> JUDGE OTIS: What kind of expense?
> MR. BENNETTS: Logging.
> MR. PATTERSON: And now, witness, as to whether that amount was charged on the same day, July 6, 1925, to the special bond investment account.
> MR. BENNETTS: The charge was made in the special bond investment account on the same date, July 6, 1925.

The prosecution followed with 32 other items that were charged to the same special bond investment account. Bennetts' testimony showed that the entire $133,922.61 went for such things as logging, surveying, engineering and construction expenses, and for the expense of obtaining options on land in the reservoir area of the proposed Bagnell Dam on behalf of the Missouri Hydro-Electric Power Company. Those transactions were negotiated through the Kansas City Finance Company.

A surprise witness brought to Kansas City by the government was none other than Guy Huston who had been tied to Cravens in several bond deals and the promotion of land bank stock in the eastern states. Huston was under a nine-year prison sentence in connection with fraudulent transactions at the Southern Minnesota Joint Stock Land Bank. Huston had served as fiscal agent for the Kansas City Joint Stock Land Bank. He identified two drafts drawn on his account by Cravens. One draft was for $52,000, the other for $8000, The drafts represented Huston's debt to the Kansas City Joint Stock Land Bank through the purchase of stock, but were deposited in Cravens' personal account. J.E. Huston, brother of Guy Huston, and Miss Margaret Smith of New York also testified to the authenticity of the drafts.

When the prosecution concluded their case against Cravens and Miss Todd concerning the first 33 counts of the indictment, Conrad came forth with his "magic pill,' remedy for the situation. Four days after the last expenditure of the 33 counts, Conrad told the court and the jury, the Special Bond Investment Account was liquidated by the payment of $495,715.30 plus interest and bond premium to total $497,492.64 in a check to the land bank.

The government called Lester C. Manson, Washington, D.C., an attorney for the Land Banks Association. This set off another lively jousting between Dodds and Conrad. Conrad said Manson couldn't testify about what he and Cravens and Miss Todd discussed as he was their attorney and it would be like, "Revealing the secrets of a client." After the court convened that particular morning, nine days after the beginning of the trial, Judge Otis ruled that Manson had been the attorney for the land bank and not for Walter Cravens nor Miss Todd. Manson was directed to answer any questions concerning conversations he may have had with either Cravens or Miss Todd.

Manson said that Cravens had contacted him by long distance telephone and had asked him to come to Kansas City on behalf of the bank in securing or attempting to secure the approval by the Farm Loan Board of a proposed issue of $600,000 ($7,290,000) of bonds. Manson said that the Board was refusing to approve the bond issue that involved a question of whether the bank was solvent and whether the officers had misappropriated or misapplied the bank's funds. Manson told the jury that, "It occurred to me after discussing the matter with Mr. Cravens that his interests might be diverse from the interests of the bank."

Manson laid out the convoluted scheme used by Cravens and signed on to by Alice B. Todd that resulted in an increase in capital stock in the land bank issued to Cravens for the full amount of $497,715.30. Involved were loans made by Cravens from various banks in Chicago, New York, Kansas City and St. Louis in the amount of $850,000, the securing of government bonds and cash amounting to $846,927.79, turning the bonds over to the Kansas City Finance Company, selling them, giving Cravens' check for $112,827.96 on his personal account in the First National Bank of Kansas City where some of the cash proceeds of the $850,000 had been deposited, and finally the finance company giving its check for $497,715.64 to the land bank. Manson and the government contended that the $497,715.64 came out of the funds really belonging to the land bank and that it completely lost the $133,922.61 to the Missouri Hydro-Electric Power Company.

In cross examination, Manson's letter to defense attorney Brewster dated March 22, 1927, was introduced in which Manson gave a favorable report on the condition of the Kansas City Joint-Stock Land Bank.

"The Kansas City Joint Stock Land Bank is not only solvent, but every dollar's worth of foreclosure real estate could be written off in full as utterly worthless without coming anywhere near affecting the solvency of the bank."

In re-direct, Dodds asked Manson when he had changed his mind about the bank from what he had written in the letter to Brewster.

"In April," Manson said, "when Mr. Cravens and Miss Todd told me the bank could not meet its interest payments."

Straw loans made by the land bank on farms already foreclosed made up many of the counts against Cravens and Alice B. Todd for false entries. A straw loan in this case was a fictitious loan standing in the name of a non-responsible person on land already acquired through foreclosure by the bank. The government said that entries under

"Loans Paid Out," were actually shown to have gone for the benefit and use of the defendants. The defense claimed the entries were mistakenly included in a list of straw loans Cravens was taking off the bank's hands and for which he had given his check and were nothing more than a rectification of this mistake.

W.F. Smith, federal land appraiser, testified that a tract of land in Dunklin County that the bank had made a "Straw loan" for $40,000 was worth only $15,933.

The defense, in a stipulation made with the prosecution, admitted the bank had engaged in the practice of "Straw Loans," but called it a common practice in the loan business. With the defense admitting the existence of the straw loans, plus the fact they had employed them, the government dismissed 70 witnesses they had called to court to establish the existence of the fake loans.

On other counts, the defense claimed the checks that ended up in Cravens account were really reimbursements for operating expenses Cravens had assumed during the early stages of the land bank when to have paid the expenses itself would have impaired its capital stock. There were, however, no entries on the bank's book to show any such liability to the bank.

Counts 55 through 60 reflected payments for which the land bank had no indebtedness and were clearly for the benefit of Cravens and the Missouri Hydro-Electric Power Company.

The prosecution, exhausted from its travails through myriad stacks of records and logs, through the testimony of 100 witnesses and 600 exhibits, rested. Now it was the turn of Walter Cravens and Alice B. Todd to tell their side of what exactly took place when the two of them made all those entries in all those ledgers.

IN DEFENSE

ON THE DAY when the defense would take the floor of the courtroom, there were no vacant seats, unlike the beginning days of the trial. The defense began with a succession of eight character witnesses for Cravens and Miss Todd. Cravens was a visionary and a skillful executive, witnesses contended, who devised the plan of organizing the Hydro-Electric Company to develop electric power for St. Louis and Kansas City and other sections of the country which would require an eventual expenditure of some thirty million dollars.

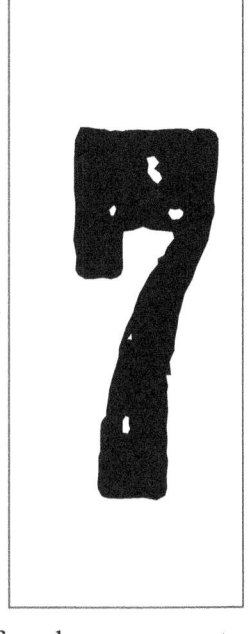

The project, the defense pointed out, made necessary the acquisition of lands along the Osage River in the state of Missouri, which would be overflowed by the construction of a dam known as Bagnell Dam. The lands, which the land bank had taken over in Missouri and Kansas as a result of foreclosure, were to be exchanged for lands in the area which would be submerged by the dam, which lands the Hydro-Electric Company would be compelled to pay for in cash. The defense was building a case that would claim if it were not for unwarranted government interference, Cravens would have worked out this situation to the benefit and possible salvation of the bank.

Witnesses told of Alice B. Todd's membership in the Kansas City Women's Chamber of Commerce and holding the office of treasurer of that organization. George H. Hubbard, real estate dealer in Versailles, MO, testified for Walter Cravens as did L.C. Staples of the H.D. Lee Mercantile Company in Salina who knew both Cravens and Miss Todd as both of them had worked for him.

The value of character witnesses would be assessed when Judge Otis addressed the jury at the end of the trial.

May 21, 1928, Miss Alice B. Todd, wearing a dark blue lace-trimmed dress and blue hat, was called to the witness stand. The prosecution and those following the case appeared to be taken by surprise. Calling Miss Todd seemed to be an indication that the defense was ready to wrap up the case.

Miss Todd was sworn in carrying a small notebook. Henry Conrad started his questioning of Miss Todd with inquiries about her earlier life, born near Salina, Kansas, attending schools in Salina elementary and two years of high school followed by a business course and employment as a stenographer at the H.D. Lee Mercantile Company in Salina. She told about her nine years in California and her subsequent employment with the Cravens Mortgage Company and finally signing on with Walter Cravens at the newly formed Liberty Joint-Stock Land Bank in Salina. In 1922, when the Kansas City Joint-Stock Land Bank, formed by Walter Cravens, took over the business of the Liberty Joint Stock Land Bank, Miss Todd told the court she was named secretary.

Conrad's questioning entered into the business of the Liberty Joint Stock Land Bank and the difficulties arising from the formation of the land bank. According to the responses of Miss Todd, a quarter of a million dollars was the necessary capital. Because none of the beginning capital could be used for operating expenses, bank directors called upon Cravens to furnish operating funds from his own pocket, she maintained.

Miss Todd referred frequently to the small book she had taken to the stand. According to the figures she read from her book, the bank owed Walter Cravens $182,000. The government's counsel objected, saying her figures in the book were compiled from bank records and were not the original records. To which Miss Todd said she could not get the bank's records as they were in the hands of the government. "I have tried repeatedly to get the books," she said.

She said that she and Cravens had designed the banks records so that they would, "Remain a monument," to their efforts.

IN DEFENSE 69

The Kansas City *Post* described Miss Todd's appearance as typical of the modern business woman. "She was businesslike in her manner and straight of bearing."

The land bank retained one percent from all the loans, Miss Todd said. The farmers paid six percent on the loans; the bondholders received five percent. Following the takeover of the Liberty Joint Stock Land Bank by the Kansas City Joint Stock Land Bank, an additional 17 million dollars in farm loans was made. She testified that at the time the government took over the bank, 45 million dollars in farm loans was on the books.

She told how the Farm Loan Act provided no system of bookkeeping for joint stock land banks and how she and Walter Cravens devised their own method of keeping the records based on their experience in banking. She was emphatic about how uniformity in bookkeeping in land banks records did not exist.

This exchange took place between Miss Todd and Conrad:

> MR. CONRAD: Miss Todd, I want to ask you this question: Tell this jury whether you at any time ever made an entry on the books or took part in any kind of character of transaction involved in these counts or otherwise with any intent to defraud this bank out of a penny of money in any way whatsoever?
>
> MISS TODD: I did not.
>
> MR. CONRAD: Did you know of your own personal knowledge of any act or anything done by Mr. Cravens, of the receipt of any money by him in reference to or from this bank with the intention in any way of depriving or defrauding this bank of a penny?
>
> MISS TODD: I certainly do not.
>
> MR. CONRAD: Tell the jury whether or not you yourself, or of your own knowledge, there was ever any entry made upon the books of this bank at any time for the purpose of deceiving any person whomsoever?

> MISS TODD: No, sir.
>
> MR. CONRAD: Do you know of any entry having been made by any person, including Mr. Cravens, or his knowledge of any transaction which had for its purpose deceiving any individual whether farm loan examiner or whosoever he might be, of deceiving him in any respect whatsoever?
>
> MISS TODD: I do not.

Miss Todd continued to maintain that any records of the land bank that was not understandable to the examiners was because errors in bookkeeping had been adjusted by other entries to correct them and not with fraudulent intent.

Roscoe Patterson rose to begin the cross-examination. As he approached Miss Todd, she showed him a slight smile. He began his questioning with details about her salary at the land bank. That line of inquiry was halted by the court declaring a recess. The prosecution's grilling of Miss Alice B. Todd would have to wait.

When court convened again, Nugent Dodds, counsel for the prosecution, took up the subject of Miss Todd's salary history. From 1918 to 1921 Miss Todd was paid $75 a month. In 1922, after being named treasurer of the Kansas City Joint-Stock Land Bank, her salary jumped to $200 a month. In 1923 her salary became $3600 that year, but the books showed additional payments of $5300. In 1924 she was to be paid $4800 she said, but the books showed her receiving $6965. In 1925 she said her salary was $6500, but again, the books gave a larger amount of $7150. In 1922, Miss Todd deposited $165,123.05 into her personal bank account. She explained by stating that the account was used by Cravens and the Cravens Mortgage Company and that some of the account was trust funds. When she underwent an operation, the bank advanced the money to pay her hospital bill. The defense raised several objections to Dodds' line of questioning:

> MR. BREWSTER I say this, that in fairness, the jury is entitled to know that the Government does not claim to have any evidence tending to show that any

of the money in Miss Todd's bank account came out of the bank. I think that is only fair. I think counsel ought to just state it.

MR. DODDS: In answer to that, I would say to the Court that the purpose of this testimony is to have this witness, who has testified that she was poor and had a small income for several years—$75 a month up to that time in 1922, and thereafter only a salary, she stated it—the purpose is to show how it is that her personal bank account shows an annual income of several thousand . . .

MISS TODD: It has been stated that I testified I was a poor girl. I didn't so testify.

Miss Todd went on to explain the unusual deposits in her personal account as coming from relatives' trust fund, her savings from a nine year job in California and from Cravens using her personal account for deposits going to the Kansas City Finance company from time to time.

When Dodds got to Miss Todd's 1926 salary of $8700, the court sustained Conrad's objection to the entire line of questioning of Miss Todd's salary and the testimony was stricken from the record.

The counsel for the prosecution read Miss Todd's note to Cravens dated November 7, 1924:

"Mr. Cravens: There are certain little matters that should be closely watched in connection with the preparation of the report to the government. I personally went over the figures this month with Mr. Miller and I am sure the report is all right. What I refer to particularly are the items which we are holding in a more or less suspended account. For instance your personal checks in payment of the Wichita stock matters are being held by Mr.. Siler, the money, of course, having been shown on our books as deposited in the First National Bank at Kansas City account and it is not as a matter of fact in that account."

Asked by the prosecution what she meant by, "little matters to be closely watched," she said, "Any suspense matter should be closely watched by a business executive."

Dodds then centered his inquiry on a sum of $221,351.44 reported to the Farm Loan Board as being on deposit in the First National Bank in Kansas City was not in fact deposited there. This line of questioning took place:

> MR. DODDS: When you reported to the Farm Loan Board that there was $221,000 ($2,685,150) odd dollars on deposit in the First National Bank of Kansas City, $221,351.44, that was not actually on deposit in the First National Bank of Kansas City, was it, Miss Todd?
>
> MISS TODD: The amount was not actually on deposit in the First National Bank of Kansas City, on that date.
>
> MR. DODDS: And it wasn't on this date that you made the report to the Board, was it?
>
> MISS TODD: Probably not.
>
> MR. DODDS: It wasn't when you made the report of November 24?
>
> MISS TODD: I think not.

Dodds and Miss Todd then engaged in a lengthy controversy wherein Miss Todd refused to admit any false statement in the report or in the entry. Dodds repeatedly asked Miss Todd directly whether the entry she had spoken of as being put in the report by her of the deposit in the First National Bank of Kansas City was a true or false entry, she refused again to answer directly.

> JUDGE OTIS: The witness can certainly answer if she drew up this report, whether the statement contained therein is true or false.
>
> MR. CONRAD: Exception, please.
>
> JUDGE OTIS; Noted.
>
> MR. DODDS: (To Miss Todd) The court says for you to state whether this statement was true or false.
>
> JUDGE OTIS: It is one or the other.

MISS TODD: The statement is incorrect, based on the books.

MR. DODDS: I didn't ask you that. I asked you whether the statement in the book was true or false. Answer it please. I insist on an answer.

JUDGE OTIS: Answer the question, Miss Todd. The words false and true are simple words and the defendant should know whether or not the entry is false or true.

MR. DODDS: You were the secretary of the bank.

MISS TODD: The statement was incorrect.

MR. DODDS: The witness hasn't answered the question, may it please the court.

JUDGE OTIS: (To Miss Todd) answer the question.

MISS TODD: May I ask Your Honor a question?

JUDGE OTIS: Yes.

MISS TODD: After I have answered this question, may I explain it?

JUDGE OTIS: Yes.

MR. DODDS: Answer it.

MR. CONRAD: Exception.

MR. DODDS: Is the statement made therein, true or false?

MISS TODD: The statement may be admitted to be false as reflecting the actual deposit—

MR. DODDS: Now, Miss Todd—

MR. CONRAD: (Interrupting) We object to him interfering with the answer, now.

JUDGE OTIS: Yes.

MISS TODD: But the bank held in its possession not only Mr. Cravens' check for the amount, but the collateral pledged to that check of value equal to the sum shown on deposit.

But the damage to the defense, Miss Todd and Cravens had been done. She had admitted making a false entry in the land bank's books and to knowing that it was false, the very accusation the prosecution had been pursuing throughout its presentation. The false entry charges totaled 42 counts involving $748,788.08. The statute covering false entries in the crime of misapplying the funds of a land bank states:

"A wrongful misapplication of funds, even if made in the hope or belief that the bank's welfare would ultimately be promoted, is none the less a violation of the statute, if the necessary effect is or may be to injure or defraud the bank."

TUESDAY, MAY 22,

MAKES ADMISSION

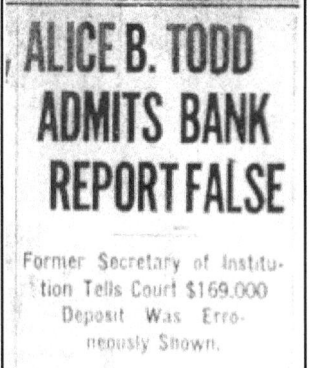

ALICE B. TODD ADMITS BANK REPORT FALSE

Former Secretary of Institution Tells Court $169,000 Deposit Was Erroneously Shown.

Alice B. Todd recognized the significance of her testimony. Judge Otis adjourned the trial a half-hour early because of the strain on the witness.

The air seemed taken out of the sails of the defense. Their next move was putting Walter Cravens himself on the stand. You could bet that the eyes of any farmers were on the slick looking banker in his expensive suit. They of the plain cloth, chambray shirts, denim trousers and flour sack dresses craned for a good look at the man who was handling millions of dollars while they barely had food on their table. By this time, at the beginning of the Great Depression, bankers had the role of the bad guys. And here was one that had finally been caught up with. They had to have been straining forward to hear what he had to say in his defense.

But the defense soft-pedaled on Cravens testimony. It was obvious that Conrad and his companions in defense counsel had planned on Miss Todd's denial of any wrong doing to be the foundation of Cravens' defense as well as Miss Todd's. In fact, the defense counsel put it this way to Cravens, "The counts in this indictment from the first to the last have been covered by the testimony of Miss Todd." Cravens agreed.

Cravens continued to insist, reiterating the statements of Miss Todd, that the land bank owed him $182,000 ($2,211,300). He claimed the checks represented to be irregular were drawn upon his own private account.

Dodds went after Cravens about the hiring of a law firm to bring suit against Guy Huston and paying for that lawsuit out of bank funds.

> MR. DODDS: The claim was one by you personally against Guy Huston for damages in a certain sum by reason of the fact of your claim Huston hadn't come across with money that he had agreed to.
>
> MR. CRAVENS: That firm performed two different services.
>
> MR. DODDS: One was for the hydro and one was for you?
>
> MR. CRAVENS: Both were for the hydro.
>
> MR. DODDS: One was for the hydro itself and one was for you . . . regardless of what you may have intended to do with the proceeds.
>
> MR. CRAVENS: Yes, but it was for the benefit of the hydro company.

Trial watchers continued to scratch their heads on just why Miss Todd had led off the defense and Cravens seemed to be asked only about her testimony and little about his actions.

During the summation to the jury, they heard about two Walter Cravens, one pictured by Roscoe Patterson as a, "Shrewd, unscrupulous Get-Rich-Quick Wallingford," who used bank funds to promote his own enterprise, the Missouri Hydro Electric Power Company.

Cravens was compelled to falsify the bank records, Patterson told the jury, in order to conceal his operations.

"Walter Cravens gambled with the money of the stockholders and the bondholders, and attempted to cover up his operations by juggling the accounts of the bank. The records show that in a period of a few months the bank advanced the power company approximately $134,000 ($1,634,000) and there is not the scratch of a pen on bank books to show it."

In summation, Patterson asked the jury, "How did they balance it? They balanced it with a check for $497,000. And where did the money come from? Where did they get it? They got it by issuing duplicate certificates of stock in the sum, I believe, of one million dollars wasn't it?"

Miss Todd and Cravens sat close together at a counsel table during Patterson's summation. They frequently leaned closer and whispered to the other. Miss Todd at times busily wrote on a tablet.

Patterson dwelt on the letter Cravens had written to Guy Huston in which Cravens said he had worked out an agreement with Bickel, the contractor, in which Bickel would build the dam at Bagnell that the Hawley Company had designed and that, as builder, Bickel would keep one third of the ten percent profit on the building cost and Cravens and Huston would split the remaining profit.

"I say secret arrangement, and I will state to you in just a moment why it was a secret arrangement. He tells him that by this secret arrangement, Bickel is only to receive one-third of the ten percent and the other two-thirds is to go to Guy Huston and Walter Cravens . . . he told Huston, 'I am directing this to your home because I don't want it to go into your files.' Now was he working for the interest of the Land Bank when he entered into that sort of an arrangement or was he working for the interest of Walter Cravens in trying to satisfy the itching palm at the expense of his bank.?"

When Conrad and Brewster rose to give closing arguments, the jury heard about an entirely different Walter Cravens. They heard about a man Conrad said was in his middle stage of life, broken by the valiant effort he had made to save the bank from destruction, and facing prison because of the sacrifice he had made attempting to realize his life's ambition.

The defense was stuck with their original argument that Cravens had, by forming the Missouri Hydro-Electric Power Company, come up with a creative means of using the frozen assets from foreclosed farm loans in acquiring land for the electric company's use, all of which was in the province and responsibilities of the president of the bank.

Concerning the building of the dam, Brewster declared that Cravens saw in the hydro-electric development the creation of a lake as large as one of the Great Lakes, with a vast amount of electrical power resulting. He described the project as having as much "effect on the future destinies of this state as did the laying of rails across its hills and prairies."

"The government," Brewster told the jury, "would have you believe it was a crime to make a contract with the Missouri Hydro Electric Company. The land bank, or any other bank, has the right to make a contract that results in gain for the bank."

The two major reasons for the action against Cravens and Miss Todd, the defense alleged, were the enemies deliberately trying to wreck Cravens' bank so they could gain control and that any misleading entries in the banks books were nothing more than errors, caused by the lack of direction from the Farm Loan Board, and had been corrected in later entries.

As evidence of the government's obsession to get Cravens, defense attorney R.R. Brewster pointed out that the Attorney General had sent his top man all the way from Washington to prosecute Cravens.

"Out of millions of transactions, the government picked out 88 in an attempt to prove these two defendants guilty of wrong doing," Conrad said.

"We do not want mercy for Alice Todd and Walter Cravens," the defense told the jury. "All we ask for is justice . . . We must go into the hearts and minds to get a motive for a crime. If there is no motive, there is no crime."

Conrad made a plea for womanhood on behalf of Miss Todd who frequently dabbed at her eyes with a handkerchief. Cravens displayed the same calm disposition he had throughout the trial.

The court presented the case to the jury and charged them as follows:

"The contention is, as you have heard it put to you, that these alleged misapplications were not misapplications at all, but that they were repayments to Mr. Cravens of sums that were due him by the bank. Did the Joint Stock Land Bank owe Mr. Cravens a sum of money in excess at least of the amount referred to in these counts, dealing with the subject of misapplication? With reference to counts 76 to 88 inclusive, which charge false entries, if you find and believe that false entries were made by the defendants, that they were false in the sense in which that term has hitherto been defined by the Court, and that they were made with the intention of defrauding the bank or to deceive the agents of the Government or examiners of the bank, then in that event, if these facts have been proved beyond a reasonable doubt, you will find the defendants guilty"

The judge brought up the reputation factor. "There is evidence in this case touching on the good reputation of these defendants. That evidence is to be considered by you in this case. The law presumes that a man or woman who had a good reputation is less likely to commit a crime than one who does not have a good reputation, but if, after considering all the evidence in this case, including that touching on the subject of good reputation, you believe the defendants to be guilty beyond a reasonable doubt, it is your duty to find them guilty even though you find the evidence shows they had a good reputation. If their good reputation raises in your minds a reasonable doubt as to the guilt of the defendants, then your verdict should be not guilty."

The sixteen-day trial was over. At 2:45 o'clock on May 23, 1928 the fate of Walter Cravens and Alice B. Todd was handed over to a jury of twelve men. The jury foreman was J.E. Dunbar a real estate dealer from Kansas City. The other jurors were: S. S. Brown, laborer, Kingston, Caldwell County; C. C. Carder, real estate, Kansas City; N. G. Gish, farmer, Tiffen, St. Clair County; A. C. LeFaver, motor car dealer, Malta Bend, Saline County; C. E. Morris, barber, Kansas City; Richard Pence, engineer, Buckner, Jackson County; Frank A. Parker, bank employee, Kansas City; A. H. Fulham, salesman, Kansas City; M. I. Rothschild, salesman, Kansas City; T. W. Houston, insurance, Kansas City; L. W. Derrick, salesman, Kansas City. Evening came and the jury had not reached a verdict. They were permitted to separate for the night. An anxious night for Walter Cravens and Alice B. Todd.

The battle was done; the man who rode the rocket to meteoric heights, the servile bookkeeper who was there at every step, by his side, signing checks, making the book entries, smiling down at her questioners. And the examiners who walked into the 12th floor, elaborate offices in the land bank building, wearing guns. Who would be left standing when the jury came back in?

At 12:00 o'clock noon on the following day the jury announced they had reached a verdict.

THE VERDICT

BY 12:30, MAY 24, Walter Cravens, his wife Bertha, Alice B. Todd and their counsel, Henry Conrad and C.H. Kohler, arrived at the courtroom after being summoned by the bailiff on Judge Otis's direction. Together they took the elevator to the floor of the courtroom. Miss Todd paused before entering the courtroom and touched a powder puff to her face.

Cravens' family and friends of Miss Todd were seated in the spectators' section and her friends patted her on the back as she entered. The two, along with their counsel, sat at the defendants' table. Cravens sat impassively, his elbows on the table. Miss Todd sat straight, her lips compressed.

At the prosecutors' table, Roscoe Patterson and Nugent Dodds waited. Their hope had to be that the jury would find Cravens and Miss Todd guilty on at least one of the 88 counts against them. Two and a half years had passed since the crew of examiners under S. G. Bennetts had barged into the Land Bank building on 15th Street in downtown Kansas City armed, not just with complaints of corruption from numerous investors, but with guns. Hundreds, even thousands of hours had been spent by the examiners rumbling through the maze of records created by Cravens and Miss Todd and an equal number of hours by Dodds and others in preparing the cases for three grand juries. Now the 88 counts of criminality were in the hands and minds of 12 men. Just one count of guilty, at least one, they both had to be hoping.

At the other table, great trepidation must have settled on Miss Todd and Walter Cravens. Whereas the government people at the table across the aisle from them had only time and effort to lose, Miss Todd and Cravens had lives and careers at risk. Cravens was, no doubt, chagrinned at the outcome of his many efforts to keep his land bank alive. Was he blaming Miss Todd for his predicament? It had to register in his mind that it was she who had admitted on the witness stand that she had made a false entry in the bank's books, an admission of guilt. What more could a jury ask for?

Alice B. Todd, of course, knew that her fantastic rise from bookkeeper to secretary of the country's second largest joint-stock land bank was at an end. Even if they were to be acquitted, there was practically no hope that Cravens would ever get his bank back from the receivers. That possibility was over. What lay ahead for her, guilty or not guilty was uncertainty.

The jury returned and took their seats. The courtroom was hushed. A number of farmers and others who had been following the trial had trickled back into the courtroom after the word had spread; the jury had reached a verdict.

"All rise," the bailiff announced, and Judge Merrill Otis entered. He asked jury foreman J. E. Dunbar if a decision had been reached. When Dunbar answered in the affirmative, the judge ordered the verdicts sent up to him. Two thick packets of papers, relating to each of the defendants, was passed to the judge and he looked them over, one by one, then handed them to Harry C. Spaulding, deputy clerk. The judge directed Spaulding to read the verdicts.

Spaulding read the verdict of Count One against Walter Cravens: guilty. He flipped through the papers, scanning the verdicts for each of the 88 counts.

Looking at the judge, Spaulding announced, "They are all the same, your honor."

Judge Otis told Spaulding he could announce them together if the defense had no objections. Conrad announced that the defense had no objections to waiving the reading of each verdict individually. On each of the 88 counts against Walter Cravens, the verdict of the jury was guilty, Spaulding announced. Cravens sat impassively at the table with no visible emotion. Spaulding moved on to the jury's verdict on the 88 counts against Alice B. Todd. The verdicts were the same as for Cravens, guilty on all counts. Miss Todd's face flushed at the announcement and the lines about her mouth tightened as she assumed a more erect position in her chair.

Roscoe Patterson showed astonishment as he turned to look at his prosecuting companions. Nugent Dodds showed equal surprise. Obviously, the prosecution had not dared hope for such a complete victory.

Judge Otis thanked the jury, complimenting them on their patience and attention throughout the 16 days of trial. He said he was aware of the difficulty in sitting through the presentation of involved questions of finances and bookkeeping. He then discharged the jury.

The judge told the defendants that sentence would be passed on them at 9:30 the following Monday. Conrad and the others on the defense team said they would have the necessary papers for an appeal prepared by the following Monday. The judge told the defendants that following the sentence, they could be released on appeal bonds.

The maximum sentence that could be imposed on Cravens and Miss Todd was five years in the federal prison on each count, or $5000 fine, or both. The minimum would be a fine of $1 or one day in jail or both.

The defendants were mindful that they were under indictment from the other two grand juries. Nugent Dodds said those would be called for trial in due time. He expressed doubt, though, that any further court action would be scheduled until the outcome of any appeal by Cravens and Miss Todd was concluded.

The defendants went to the spectators' section and talked with relatives and friends. No outward display of emotion was observed on the part of anyone there.

Jury foreman J. E. Dunbar told the Kansas City *Star* that, despite the intricacies of the details of evidence, he felt the jury had a very clear grasp of the case. He called the first ballot taken a sort of "feeler" to see how the jury felt on the question of guilt or innocence. Eight jurors were for conviction, two for acquittal with two jurors doubtful.

The next ballots taken were on the individual counts against Cravens and Miss Todd. In all, about 25 ballots were taken, Dunbar said. Finally, the jurors were all in accord on guilt. Dunbar said the jurors saw the case, "Pretty much an open and shut proposition."

"We felt that the government has proved its case," he told the media gathered there. "That meant, of course, that the defense had not made any great showing."

Nugent Dodds said he was satisfied with the verdict. "I believe it is a just verdict," he said. "The government tried to be fair in the trial and I believe it was fair."

But Henry Conrad and the defense counsel team along with Walter Cravens saw it differently. Conrad had enumerated a long list of what he thought could be "reversible errors," by the court, the prosecution and by the jury. It was as if he had begun his appeal case the day Miss Todd admitted she had made a false entry in the land bank's books, knowing at the time she did it that it was indeed a false entry.

Cravens, no doubt, considering his eternal belief in what he was doing, saw it only in the vein of just another setback like so many he had been through with the mounting foreclosures and the clamoring of the bondholders and stockholders when the interest checks stopped coming their way. But for Alice B. Todd this had to be the most crushing day of her life. From the young schoolgirl walking into her first job at the mercantile company to handle their books, to the unbelievable heights of national attention, one of only two female executives in the land bank national network. And now, facing a term in prison. Looking at Walter Cravens, she had to be wondering if it had all been worth it.

One more week of freedom then a life unknown.

A FINE JUNE DAY broke at dawn on the second of the month. By 9:30 that morning, a small crowd had gathered inside the federal courthouse in Kansas City, Missouri. This was to be the day when Walter Cravens and Alice B. Todd would learn what price they would pay for their conviction of misapplying land bank funds for their own use and for making false entries in the bank's books to cover up their actions.

Judge Merrill Otis asked the defendants if they wanted to say anything to the court before he imposed sentence. Walter Cravens rose to say, "I wish to maintain my innocence and I always will. As president of the bank, I was, of course, responsible for it. I do not want to be put in the light of avoiding my responsibility"

Miss Todd, standing, told the court directly, "I have nothing to say except to affirm Mr. Cravens' statement as to his innocence and that of myself."

"You had a fair trial," Judge Otis told them. He spoke of the, "Extravagance of fairness" on the part of the government. He said, "All I know about this case is the testimony that I heard . . . ." that he, "had been convinced by the testimony that the defendants were guilty of the charges and also of the intent to violate the law."

"However," he said, "by no means is the court certain the defendants started in the beginning with the intention to defraud the bank."

Then the defense made a point of the fact that one of the jurors had served on another panel that year and said that he had not been summoned properly. Judge Otis overruled the defense motion for a new trial.

"I cannot help but believe," the judge said, "that Walter Cravens has the deeper guilt."

Judge Otis then read the sentence of Cravens. On the first forty-four counts of the indictment the sentence was five years imprisonment and on the first fifteen counts imposed a fine of $1000 on each count for a total of $15,000. On the last forty-four counts, Cravens was sentenced to one year on each count, each to be served concurrently, consecutively to the sentence on the first forty-four counts. On the last ten counts, the judge imposed a fine of $1,000 on each count for a total of $10,000, making an aggregate fine of $25,000. Cravens, as before, showed no change in emotion.

"As to the defendant, Alice B. Todd, who" Judge Otis said, "I believe is not the chief offender, by any means, in this case, who is undoubtedly a woman of extra-ordinary intelligence and except for these offenses, of fine character, and whose wrong-doing in this case, I believe from what I have seen in the trial of the case, was actuated by loyalty to the president of this bank, her employer. Perhaps, also, her benefactor in the sense that he may have given her the position which she held, although, about that, I do not know. I cannot feel that she should sustain anything like as severe punishment as should be suffered by her co-defendant in the case. The punishment she will suffer, however, is not much less, perhaps, no matter how earnestly the Court might try to modulate it. As to the defendant Alice Todd, it is the sentence and judgment of the Court that she be imprisoned in whatever penitentiary may be designated by the Attorney General of the United States for a period of one year and one day."

The defense then filed a notice of an appeal. Walter Cravens was released on $20,000 bond and Miss Todd on $5,000 bond. One of the sureties for Miss Todd was Mrs. Walter Cravens on the basis of the Cravens home at 618 West Sixty-Second Street.

Attorney Hanna, in examining Mrs. Cravens, got this response:

Q: State your full name to the Court, please.

A: Mrs. Walter Cravens, or Mrs. Bertha Cravens.

Mrs. Cravens said that the property on West 62nd Street was in her name, $27,500 ($334,125) had been paid for it and that it was now worth, in her opinion, $24,000 and had a $15,000 Building and Loan encumbrance.

Q: The equity in the property would be that?

A: Well, fifteen from twenty-four would be how much?

Q: $9,000. Do you have any other property of your own, Mrs. Cravens, other than this one you have just described?

A: No, sir.

Q: Or other wealth?

A: No, sir.

Judge Otis complimented Nugent Dodds and Roscoe Patterson for their prosecution of the trial.

Walter Cravens' sentence of six years in prison would be served at the federal prison in Leavenworth, Kansas, while Miss Todd's one year and a day would wait on whatever place, the attorney general's department would designate.

It was quite obvious that Walter Cravens was far from done. Two more sets of indictments awaited him from previous grand juries plus, that of the federal court in Ohio for using the mail to defraud stockholders in his Kansas City Joint-Stock Land Bank. And the receivers of the land bank itself, in control of the bank since April 1927, were contemplating action against him to recover lost funds. But Cravens continued to tell friends and associates that it was all one grand plot to wrest control of his bank from him. He and Conrad were talking and planning appeal, even as they departed from the Kansas City Federal Courthouse under $20,000 bond.

As for Alice B. Todd, after the bond had been made, she appeared cheerful. She smiled and said, "Well, let's go home."

What choice did she have? For ten years her fate had been tied to Walter Cravens. Facing the prospect of a year in jail had to be frightening to her. So did the very idea of going it alone, without the help of Cravens. But she was not yet to that point.

Mrs. Curran said that the property on West 62nd Street, in her books, $37,500 ($35,437.57 had been paid for it, and that it was now worth, in her opinion, $24,000 and had a $15,000 building and Loan encumbrance.

AFTER TRIAL

ALICE B. TODD went home to Salina, Kansas. No longer the highest regarded female executive in Kansas City, she returned to her roots. She had relation in Salina, people who still believed in her. People who didn't gawk at the woman who was headed to prison for a year and a day. Whatever regrets she held, she held privately. Cravens' planned appeal to the federal appellate court would include her. Still tied to the man, for better or worse. Almost like marriage.

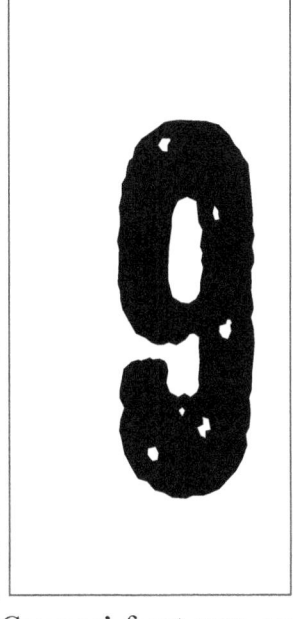

Cravens was not a man to sit idle. Besides the planned appeal, he was at work inserting himself into a settlement with the holding company that Ralph Street had worked out a contract with to take over the Missouri Hydro-Electric Power Company. Conrad was Cravens' front man on that effort, also. And it was rumored a power company called Grand Utilities was in financial trouble, but could be rehabilitated with some cash flow. And there were several downtown Kansas City real estate deals ready for a savvy investor. All he needed was a new inflow of cash.

He "borrowed" a thousand dollars from Miss Todd.

The Public Service Commission had received an inquiry in February 1927 from a firm in Chicago asking about the issuance of an order about Case Number 4633 authorizing the hydroelectric company to issue bonds and stocks for the company. The commission advised the firm that the case was in the Federal Court in Kansas City.

Street, since April of '27 when he signed the option with the Dillon, Read holding company, had averted disaster the month after with a $75,000 loan from Stone & Webster Engineering Company. The wolves were at the door, several creditors had already filed mechanics liens against the hydro-electric company and he was about to lose all that had been invested in the project, the land that had been acquired by trade for foreclosed farms in Kansas and Missouri, the buildings on the east hillside that had been constructed with money Miss Todd and Cravens had cleverly routed through a maze of obfuscation, the 16 years of effort Street had put into the project.

Street had gone before the Missouri Public Service Commission about the $75,000 loan from Stone & Webster on May 16, 1927 for permission from that body to make the loan a part of the certificate Missouri Hydro-Electric Power Company had been granted the year before. Here is part of the exchange between the commissioners, Chairman T.J. Brown, Almon Ing and B.F. Calfee, and Ralph Street with his attorney C.E. Lombardi of the Baker, Botts, Parker and Garwood firm of Kansas City representing the banking group making the $75,000 loan:

MR. STREET: We are asking this to be a temporary loan, pending the working out of the permanent financing of the project.

CHAIRMAN BROWN: Have you any testimony you want to offer?

MR. STREET: I am willing to testify about anything you want to go into with respect to it (the $75,000 loan).

CHAIRMAN BROWN: You have to support the application by proofs.

MR. STREET: I am willing to be sworn.

Ralph Wood Street, a witness of lawful age, being first duly sworn, upon his oath, testified in behalf of the applicant (the Missouri Hydro-Electric Power Company) as follows:

CHAIRMAN BROWN: You are asking for $75,000 loan, 600 shares of no par common stock. What have you got to secure this loan?

MR. STREET: We are offering a deed of trust upon the assets of the company, which consist of 75 acres of ground at the dam site on which the construction camp is now built in part. That construction camp consists of one permanent building known as the Engineers' Quarters building, which was built to house the engineers' organization during construction, and for operators afterwards; an office building which is a temporary structure, another quarter building for the office force; a mess hall with a capacity of 300 people; three foremen's bunk houses, one laborers' bunk house; a temporary power house; machine shop and warehouse; and a railroad right of way extending from the end of the Missouri Pacific tracks at Bagnell to the dam site.

CHAIRMAN BROWN: Is that all set out in the mortgage?

MR. STREET: Yes sir.

CHAIRMAN BROWN: Anything further you have to offer, Mr. Street?

MR. STREET: I think that is our story.

CHAIRMAN BROWN: Did you have anything, Mr. Lombardi?

MR. LOMBARDI: No, sir.

MR. STREET: Mr. Lombardi represents the bankers who are making the loan.

CHAIRMAN BROWN: Who is the loan to?

MR. STREET: Making it to a bearer note.

CHAIRMAN BROWN: Making it to bearer?

MR. STREET: Yes, sir.

CHAIRMAN BROWN: Who is the mortgage made to? You have got to have somebody's name on the mortgage.

MR. STREET: (To Lombardi) Who is put in there as trustee?

MR. LOMBARDI: As the application is now filed, there is no trustee named, but we have intended to make the First National Bank of Kansas City as trustee.

CHAIRMAN BROWN: I got the wrong impression. I presumed this was a loan of Stone & Webster.

MR. LOMBARDI: Well, that is the understanding, that Dillon and Read, and Stone & Webster, will, if the commission grants the proper authority, make this advance.

CHAIRMAN BROWN: But neither the note nor the mortgage is made to them. Is a copy of the mortgage filed here?

MR. LOMBARDI: Yes, sir, attached to the application.

COMMISSIONER ING: You say it is the understanding that Stone & Webster will do what?

MR. LOMBARDI: Will make the advance of $75,000 on demand note.

COMMISSIONER ING: Between whom does that understanding exist?

LOMBARDI: Between the Missouri Hydro-Electric Company and Dillon and Read, and Stone & Webster, Inc.

COMMISSIONER ING: What is to be done with this money?

MR. STREET: It is to be used first to take up the mechanics liens which have now been reduced to judgment.

COMMISSIONER ING: Mechanics liens that have been reduced to judgment?

MR. STREET: The assignments of those judgments are deposited in escrow with the First National Bank of Kansas City, and the proceeds of this loan are to be used first to take up those assignments of judgment and the balance is to be used to pay the general creditors other than Mr. Cravens and myself.

COMMISSIONER ING: What do you mean by other than Mr. Cravens and yourself? Who does that include?

MR. STREET: Material bills, engineering fees, it is all set forth in the balance sheet which we filed.

COMMISSIONER ING: It is all shown on the balance sheet?

MR. STREET: Yes, sir.

COMMISSIONER CALFEE: What is the amount of the loan?

MR. STREET: $75,000.

COMMISSIONER CALFEE: Secured by a mortgage?

MR. STREET: Yes, sir.

COMMISSIONER CALFEE: How long is it to run?

MR. STREET: It is a demand note and the idea is to run pending the time they are making further investigations and final plans for the completion of this hydro-electric project.

COMMISSIONER CALFEE: This isn't a part of any permanent financing?

MR. STREET: No, it is a temporary financing to carry the situation pending the working out of final plans, at which time we will again be before you with permanent plans. This note isn't going to the public in any way. They are taking it up.

CHAIRMAN BROWN: I think this application ought to be a supplemental to the one heretofore filed and partially heard.

MR. LOMBARDI: If you will please give us permission we will be glad to amend the application and make it a supplemental application in the other case (Case Number 4633, wherein the hydro-electric company was asking for permission to issue stock and sell bonds to finance the Bagnell Dam project.)

CHAIRMAN BROWN: Just let the record show it is a supplemental application.

MR. LOMBARDI: I think the former application was in Case Number 4633.

CHAIRMAN BROWN: Let the record show it a supplemental application to Case Number 4633. If there is nothing further, this hearing will be submitted on the record.

Case Number 4633 was the case that Street had been having difficulty with since the funding had dried up for the project in 1926. Street and Donald Fitch had gone before the commission once before with a plan that involved a Delaware company called Super Power. Nothing came of that plan. Two days after the meeting in which Lombardi and Street appeared before the commission about the $75,000 loan from Stone & Webster, Street wrote to the commission the following:

I notice that one of the papers, in referring to the application which we filed with you on Monday (May 16, 1927) of this week, stated that we intended to sell the stock we were asking your approval for issuing. I do not recall that I made any explanation regarding this stock, but am pleased to advise that when authorized it is to be deposited in escrow in the First National Bank, to be held by it as escrow during the life of our contract with Stone and Webster, Inc. and Dillon, Read & Co., and that we have no intention of offering the stock for sale to the public . . . .

The original certificate for Convenience and Necessity granted to the Missouri Hydro-Electric Power Company on January 26, 1926 was for a period of two years. On January 20, 1928, Street filed an application for an extension to that certificate. A hearing was set for March, 12, 1928.

About 25 Linn Creek residents attended the hearing. Speaking for them and against the renewal of a certificate were attorneys Sid Roach and Charles Morrow. Roach made what J. W. Vincent in the *Reveille* called a, "manly and able protest against permitting existing chaotic conditions, under pretext of extension, continuance of other excuse for further delay."

Presiding Commissioner Brown said that if the former certificate was still alive, as contended by the applicants, no order of the commission would make it any more alive. If dead, it would remain dead, regardless of any order which the commission might make.

Street withdrew the application for an extension.

Even with the option Street signed with Dillon, Read and Company and Stone & Webster, there was no assurance that the project would actually go forward. The judgments on the mechanics liens had been taken care of with the $75,000 from Stone & Webster. Their vice president, A. L. Snyder, had been working to line up a deal to keep the dam project alive. He had successfully taken over the Conowingo project on the Susquehanna River when it had been in a similar state. He worked now with the Union Electric Light and Power Company in St. Louis who was looking for additional power to supply to the St. Joseph Lead Company operating lead mines in southeast Missouri. The Stone & Webster engineers were busy studying the dam design that the Hawley Company had completed for the project and determining what engineering changes would be required to meet the demands of Union Electric.

News trickled out about changes in the height of the dam and eventually reached Linn Creek. Residents of that town had practically resigned themselves to destruction when the Public Service Commission approved the Certificate for Convenience and Necessity in 1926. Then came the revelations of, first the takeover of Cravens' Kansas City Joint Stock Land Bank by the government, then the trial of Cravens and Miss Todd. Both events signaled a reprieve for Linn Creek, but not for long. Worry set in for county officials. Many residents of the county had already moved on, having traded their bottomland for farms elsewhere in Kansas or Missouri. A large portion of the fertile land in the valleys along the rivers and creeks feeding into the Osage lay fallow. Tax revenues declined. Schools were hurting for operating expenses. When the news about a larger dam and a new hearing before the Public Service Commission reached town, the movement against flooding them drove the opposition to re-arm with more aggressive protests.

A day after the commission received the application from Street for an extension on the certificate, J.W. Vincent wrote the commission that, "Damage already done is incalculable and further promotion will prolong a condition which has long been well nigh intolerable."

Vincent, on the subject of moving the county seat from Linn Creek, wrote this, "There seems hardly even a remote probability of the county seat being removed from this point unless by some fraudulent scheme of colonization or bribery, for the reason, if for no others, that the different sections have never even approached an agreement as to a probable site." He concluded with, "This is so vital a matter with us that even the suspense is almost equivalent to a blight upon the entire community."

In February, Jay Holst of Barnett wrote the commission about raising the height of the dam and the damage that could do to tiff mines he was working 10 or 15 miles upriver.

Robert Webb, saying he was now in business in Linn Creek after selling his property in Zebra, wrote that, "My old neighborhood

STONE & WEBSTER
(Incorporated)

CHARLES A. STONE   EDWIN S. WEBSTER
    RUSSELL ROBB   HENRY G. BRADLEE
FREDERICK P. ROYCE   GEORGE O. MUHLFELD
    HENRY B. SAWYER   FREDERICK S. PRATT
HARRY H. HUNT   HOWARD L. ROGERS

DESIGN steam power stations, hydro-electric developments, transmission lines, city and interurban railways, gas and chemical plants, industrial plants, warehouses and buildings.

CONSTRUCT either from their own designs or from designs of other engineers or architects.

MANAGE public utility and industrial companies.

REPORT on going concerns, proposed extensions and new projects.

FINANCE industrial and public utility properties and conduct an investment banking business.

is largely abandoned. Farm improvements are getting dilapidated, farms run down, roads neglected, schools have suffered greatly and the village of Zebra is deserted."

The Linn Creek Community Club, the town's chamber of commerce, wrote to the commission asking permission to attend the hearing for the hydroelectric company's extension of the certificate of convenience and necessity in the hope that, "Further vexatious delays and ruinous losses may be avoided." They outlined in the letter their opposition to the project and how it would affect Camden County. The letter was signed by W. M. Tomkins, president of the club.

In March, T. R. Foster, acting mayor of Linn Creek and chairman of the Village Board, wrote on stationary of the Linn Creek Community Club, that, "For a distance of about one hundred and twenty-five miles along these streams (Osage and Niangua Rivers) production, taxable wealth and trade have declined about one-half in the last three years. Schools have suffered so greatly that hundreds of pupils are one, two or three grades behind with their work. Many valuable farms have greatly depreciated from neglect; improvements are falling into decay, some lying idle and others poorly farmed. This in turn is a double loss to public revenue. On land optioned to the promoters, owners were forbidden to dispose of their own timber while on the other hand, thousands of dollars worth have been slashed down on the pretext of building coffer dams, and left to rot on the ground without any remuneration to the owners."

The commission filed another document from Linn Creek citizens on the same day the hydroelectric company's hearing was scheduled for an extension of their certificate. John M. Farmer, J. W. Vincent, A. M. Pope, Charles E. Morrow, C. R. Calkin, Camden County Presiding Commissioner Leonard Franklin and the Linn Creek Community Club contracted the same noted attorneys, Sid Roach and Charles Morrow, to present the commission with their protest and to represent them at the hearing.

The contents of the document stressed the remonstrators' objection to the project because "the Missouri Hydro-Electric Power

Company applicants have not complied and cannot comply with the provisions of the laws of the State of Missouri appertaining to its certificate of convenience and necessity for the reason that operations and construction under said permit have been abandoned for a period of more than one year . . . and has attempted to convey and assign its franchise, property and rights under said permit without consent and approval of this honorable commission." Further, they stated that, "Missouri Hydro-Electric Power Company is insolvent and financially unable to promote the enterprise of constructing the dam heretofore mentioned."

The company's proceedings, the remonstrators stated, "have been contrary to and against public interests and have resulted in the depreciation of property values, the suspension and stagnation of public business and private improvements, the closing of public schools, the suspension of the public road building program, and has generally proven inimical to public interests."

The remonstrators did not have the opportunity to present their protests in person to the commission on that date. Ralph Street requested permission to withdraw the supplemental application, filed January 26, 1928, which was granted by the commission.

Walter Cravens' problems deepened when the June, 1928 term of the District Court of the United States for the District of Massachusetts formed a grand jury that on September 5 returned an indictment against him and seven others charging use of the mails to defraud and for conspiracy in the sale of stocks in his Kansas City Joint-Stock Land Bank. On September 25, Roscoe Van Valkenburgh, assistant United States attorney, swore to a complaint against Cravens based on a certified copy of that indictment, before James S. Summers, U.S. commissioner. Summers then issued a warrant for Cravens arrest.

On September 10 in that already fateful year for Alice B. Todd, her mother Emeline died at the age of 79. She was buried in Salina in the Gypsum Hill Cemetery where her husband and Alice Barbara Todd's father, Andrew was buried.

The year 1928 closed with Ralph Street holding an almost done deal in his pocket from Stone & Webster along with Dillon, Read and Company with the Union Electric Light and Power Company in St. Louis for his interests in the Osage River Project. Alice B. Todd faced a year and a day in the United States Industrial Institution for women at Alderson, West Virginia and Walter Cravens was looking at six years in the federal prison at Leavenworth, Kansas.

JANUARY 19, 1929 **HERMAN LANGWORTHY** found the bondholders' committee for the Kansas City Joint-Stock Land Bank appearing before the Federal Farm Loan Board for their approval of a reorganization plan. Massey Holmes, a Kansas City attorney, represented the bondholders' protective Committee and Herman Langworthy, the receiver in charge of the Land Bank appeared. The bondholders presented a plan to the board who listened to representatives from the stockholders also.

"If the plan is approved," Langworthy told the Kansas City *Star* and *Times* Washington Bureau, "the bank will be reorganized and continue to operate."

While the Farm Loan Board wrestled with the details of trying to straighten out the finances of Cravens' land bank, Van Valkenburgh and Nugent Dodds who was prominent in the government's case against Cravens the year before, were presenting their case before James S. Summers, U.S. commissioner, for the removal of Cravens to Massachusetts to stand trial there.

The indictment in Massachusetts accused Cravens and seven others of forming farm loan companies in which worthless stock was traded to farmers in return for their land. Originally, the case against Cravens in particular contended that thirty-five statements of the Missouri-Kansas Farms Company filed in 1926 with the blue-sky commission at Massachusetts purported to show assets of $233,000 when the assets in reality were only $8000, the remaining $225,000 being represented by a check which never was cashed. The government introduced a photographic copy of a letter written February 23, 1925, by Cravens to Guy Huston in New York outlining his plan of a holding company to give assistance in the operation of land banks in Kansas City, Chicago, Des Moines and Minnesota.

> "We must have some way of carrying the paper off the books of the land banks to get the desired results," the letter said. "By having one company instead of several it never would be known as to what extent each bank participated."

The government completed their case before Summers on February 2. Henry Conrad and R. R. Brewster then presented Cravens' defense against removal. Cravens, who had been free on $20,000 bond was brought into the hearing by a U.S. marshal. Cravens attorneys based their defense on the contention that no probable cause warranting his commitment had been shown to the commissioner.

Langworthy took the Kansas City Joint-Stock Land Bank puzzle to the federal court on February 16, asking them to untangle the intricate maze of manipulation by which Walter Cravens and Miss Alice B. Todd retained control of the 44 million dollar bank and kept it afloat long after its solvency was questioned by examiners.

Langworthy's petition with the court included the Cravens Mortgage Company of Salina, Kansas, the Farmers Fund, Inc. and the Missouri-Kansas Farms Company, three of Cravens far-flung empire of financial institutions. The petition asked for an accounting of $13,273,090.32 ($161,275,527) that made up thousands of items in question. Assembled into Langworthy's suit was one by the stockholders of the Missouri-Kansas Farms Corporation for $600,000 against the land bank plus a lesser amount asked for by the receiver of the Cravens Mortgage Company.

The petition to the court charged that the hundreds of illegal and improper transactions found by the examiners in the land bank's books were made to, "reflect a false statement of the earnings and condition of the bank."

"All of this," the petition stated, "was part and parcel of one general, fraudulent and illegal plan, scheme and conspiracy." The transactions between the land bank and Cravens' other companies were claimed to be, "so interwoven that their purpose and effect are not ascertainable or understandable unless analyzed together . . . because the transactions were interlocked, enmeshed and complicated."

The petition brought out the arrangement the land bank had with the mortgage company by verbal agreement, then in 1926 by written agreement by Cravens and Miss Todd in which Cravens realized more than $400,000 ($4,860,000) in commission on farm loans made by the land bank regardless of who sold the mortgage, and $137,000 ($1,664,550) as still due. It pointed out that the Farm Loan Board disapproved this agreement on January 17, 1927.

Langworthy included the "Ponzi-like scheme," by which Cravens kept the stock in his land bank above par value by using bank capital to pay dividends, and his use of "straw" or fictitious loans, aided by Miss Todd, to show false incomes on the bank's books.

The petition elaborated on the use of bank funds to finance the hydroelectric project on the Osage River.

From the March 21, 1929, issue of the Versailles *Statesman* came this bit of news:

"The long awaited Osage River dam at Bagnell, a big hydro-electric proposition, will be built according to information given the State Highway Commission. Active construction will begin about May 1. This should mean a big industrial development for Central Missouri."

The same issue carried an article about a 60 gallon distillery that was found in operation on March 20 in a secluded cave near Lamine Station.

Herman Langworthy called for a 100 percent assessment on the stockholders of the Land bank on March 23. That would amount to a double liability on the stockholders who had invested $3.8 million in the bank. The stockholders, who stood to lose all of their initial investment plus the same amount if the assessment was approved, cried foul. The cry was loud enough to be heard all the way to Washington where congressmen were getting an ear full.

The Farm Loan Board hit the stockholders with a hurtful April Fools' joke on April 1 when they approved Langworthy's request and assessed 1800 stockholders $100 a share to help make up what Langworthy said was a $6,498,812.62 ($78,960,573) deficit at the bank. The levy was against stockholders of record on May 4, 1927, the date the bank went into receivership. The Farm Loan Act provided specifically that joint stock land bank shareholders should be held individually responsible for the contracts, debts and engagements of the bank to the par value of the stock held.

In St. Louis, on April 21, 1929, the Union Electric Light and Power Company announced their plans to build a 30 million dollar hydroelectric power plant on the Osage River near Bagnell, Missouri. The deal for the permits and the land and improvements involved in the construction of the dam included the sale or lease of the Illinois and Missouri and the Mississippi River and Bonne Terre Railroads to the Missouri Pacific Railroad Company. Union Electric announced that the St. Joseph Lead Company would take more electrical current than the quarter million residential consumers in St. Louis.

Ralph Street had completed his deal with Stone & Webster and the Dillon, Read Companies. His long-held dream had new life.

In the St. Louis *Post-Dispatch* on that same day, Union Electric President Louis H. Eagan told of the plans. He said that Union Electric was acquiring the federal license, the dam site and "other necessary lands," stated at about 60,000 acres, from the Missouri Hydro-Electric Power Company of which Walter Cravens was president.

That following Friday, J.W. Vincent had this to say about Eagan's comments in his publication of the *Reveille*:

The further announcement that, "definite arrangements for financing the project have not been made," need occasion no surprise. A maximum of 300 men are to be employed and the dam is to be completed within two years. Evidently the 300 men are expected to put in a great deal of overtime. (We notice a later version of the interview in another paper places the number at 3000)

According to the Federal Power Commission, the Missouri Hydro-Electric Power Company has never had a license and title records fail to show that it ever acquired any lands except the small tract comprising the dam site. The dam company's land, to which reference is often made, was once held by the Farmers Fund, Incorporated, and upon the collapse of the Kansas City Joint Stock Land Bank, to which these lands rightfully belonged, restitution was demanded and the lands were conveyed to the bank, then and still in a receiver's hands for liquidation.

Among the announcements in the interview we find the statement that the Camden County seat will have to be relocated or abandoned. Our state constitution very explicitly provides otherwise and we notice it is still being printed.

The interview also states that "the Union Electric Company has agreed to build a new $60,000 courthouse." Who with? Who asked them? Camden County might be supposed to be interested, but nobody here knows of any such agreement or any occasion for it.

Walter Cravens must go to Boston to stand trial, U.S. Commissioner James Summers told Cravens' attorney Henry Conrad on May 4. Summers had heard the government's appeal to remove Cravens to Boston to stand trial in the Massachusetts District Court on the indictments returned by a grand jury there. Conrad, representing Cravens, had maintained the government had never presented probable cause. Summers said they had. Conrad immediately said he would file a writ of habeas corpus in a further effort to prevent removal of Cravens to Massachusetts. His case then moved to the Federal District Court where Judge Merrill Otis, the same judge who sentenced Cravens to six years in the federal penitentiary the year before, would hear his writ of habeas corpus.

The cry of the stockholders in the Kansas City Joint Stock Land Bank reached the halls of Congress on May 23 when Massachusetts Representative George R. Stobbs called for a congressional investigation of the Kansas City bank. The Federal Farm Loan Board was considering reorganization plans for the bank and Land Bank Commissioner Paul Bestor told the Kansas City *Star* Washington Bureau he saw no reason why a congressional investigation would interfere with those plans. Bestor said he knew of no organized demand for such an investigation and said the board had no information of laxness of government examination in the bank's affairs which was the basis for Stobbs' call for an investigation.

"I am led to ask for this investigation," Stobbs told the *Star*, "in response to insistent requests from men and women in Worcester and in other parts of Massachusetts who purchased bonds and stock in this bank under representation they were guaranteed by the government."

Stobbs said that if an investigation disclosed that the government was lax in its supervision and examination, then it would bear a share of moral responsibility for the failure and would lay the foundation for asking congress to authorize a reimbursement of the losses sustained by the bond and stockholders.

Two other joint stock land banks went into receivership, the Bankers Joint Stock Land Bank of Milwaukee that had more than 15 million dollars ($182,250,000) in outstanding bonds and the Ohio Joint Stock Land Bank of Cincinnati with $1,358,000 ($16,499,700) in bonds.

On June 14, 1929, the Public Service Commission of Missouri made an important announcement concerning Union Electric Light and Power Company and Bagnell Dam.

UNION ELECTRIC TAKES OVER

GENTLEMEN:
This is to advise you that the application of the Union Electric Light and Power Company to purchase and the Missouri Hydro-Electric Power Company to sell its properties pertaining to the Osage River Hydro-Electric development . . . has been filed today as Case No. 6474 and same has been set for hearing June 25, 1929.

So began the letter to Rassieur and Goodwin, attorneys for Union Electric Light and Power Company and Conrad and Durham, attorneys for Missouri Hydro-Electric Power Company from the acting secretary of the Missouri Public Service Commission on June 14, 1929. Also began the end of the long controversy surrounding the building of Bagnell Dam. Benton, Miller and Morgan Counties were in agreement with the granting of a certificate for the building of the dam. Life and business in these counties had deteriorated over the last four years since the original certificate was granted and county officials as well as the residents wanted an end to the suffering. Only Camden County and the town of Linn Creek stood in the path obstructing the completion of the largest man-made lake in the country—maybe, even, the world.

The people in Linn Creek—the ones who had not already moved on—could hardly be blamed for their bullheaded opposition. Their town faced destruction, forty feet under water. Some, however, in that divided community felt differently about the construction of the dam. Charles Davis, chairman of the Republican Central Committee of Camden County, for instance. In a letter to the commission, Davis wrote, *"I am afraid some two or three persons are intending to appear before you with some very unreasonable demands. I wish to state again that the great majority of the people along the river at this time are and will be glad of the opportunity to sell to the Union Electric Light and Power Company . . . I wish to advise that you pay no attention to any unreasonable demands and decide these questions on a reasonable basis."*

Davis could well have been speaking of his fellow Republican, J.W. Vincent, who, besides being a Republican and publishing the Linn Creek *Reveille,* represented the district in the state legislature. On June 25, Vincent and John Farmer, a Linn Creek banker, filed a motion with the PSC to dismiss Union Electric's application for a certificate. Filing with them were Leonard Franklin, presiding judge and Associate Judges Charles Jarrett and Charles Green. Their motion maintained that the PSC was without jurisdiction to try, hear and determine the granting of a certificate among other grounds for dismissal. Their motion failed to stop the hearing. A group of citizens in Linn Creek filed an answer in opposition to Union Electric's request for a certificate to build the dam. Their efforts were also futile.

Theo Rassieur, speaking for Union Electric, began the June 25 hearing with a brief synopsis of Missouri Hydro-Electric Company's option contract with Stone & Webster and Dillon, Read and Company.

"They (Stone & Webster and Dillon, Read) spent a great deal of money looking into the matter and then Union Electric stepped into the picture and after spending some thirty odd thousand dollars in making its own investigation, spent some $280,000 ($3,402,000) which was refunded to Stone and Webster and Dillon, Read & Company."

Rassieur went on to tell the Commission that, in view of their contract with the St. Joseph Lead Company, "Involving 150,000,000 kilowatt hours per year . . . probably the largest contract ever entered into with any single customer . . . we find by October, 1931, we have to be ready to deliver the service and we've got to have a new plant ready.

We are asking permission to take over this property because we are able to get it cheap."

Union Electric's president, Louis H. Egan elaborated on why they became interested in a dam on the Osage River. "The 'run of the river' plant at Keokuk, Iowa— you cannot dam the Mississippi River . . . the country there is flat. You raise the dam four or five feet and it would flood over a lot of demonstration lands and valuable lands. The only way with a steam plant is to duplicate it, you cannot make it and store it as required and that is what we would be able to do with the Osage plant."

Egan was talking about storing potential energy by impounding water in the lake that would be formed. He told the commission, "We are not asking for sympathy, this whole territory will prosper in a way beyond belief."

He said the Osage provided about ten percent of the water into the Missouri and Mississippi at their juncture and that the dam would provide flood control and, "the whole territory will benefit."

Sid Roach, the St. Louis lawyer who grew up in Linn Creek and went on to become a two-time congressman, came into the hearing representing the opposition taxpayers and citizens as well as the County Court of Camden County, asked Egan about selling power in Camden County and the rest of the immediate area around the proposed dam.

"Anybody that wants to buy power in this territory we are prepared to sell it to them and sell it at the St. Louis rate," Egan said.

Roach asked, "Just what advantage do you think that this power project would be to Camden County?"

"It will create one of the biggest scenic attractions in the Middle West," Egan told him.

"And that is all?"

"A summer resort and we think that hundreds will come there to live, and that it will bring a great deal more business and a great many more people than would ever come without it."

Roach pressed on, "That is the only advantage?"

Egan said cheap power would lead to the erection of factories and industries in the area. And that it would be worthwhile for the county to have $20,000,000 ($243,000,000) spent in their midst.

"But won't your plant be in Miller County?", Roach asked.

Egan said they would have to clear the reservoir area all the way through with camps set up and men in them for a hundred square miles.

"We estimate there will be about three thousand (workers) and we have to provide living quarters for them, sanitation, amusements and water, and all sorts of things, and it will be a big job, and we estimate that the whole thing will require tons of material to be brought in over the railroad line to the dam—it is the biggest single project ever started in this valley, and except one other, which was Muscle Shoals, a wartime measure, one of the biggest in the country."

When the subject came up of taxation on the land taken over by Union Electric for the reservoir, Ralph Street said, "The State Tax Commission takes the position that it would be taxed by them as a whole, and the value distributed between the four counties."

Roach argued that it would take a special act of the legislature to accomplish that. Street said, "It's done on the White River (Lake Taneycomo Powersite) Project."

Asked about the $200,000 Street was asking in compensation for getting the Bagnell Dam project started, Egan responded, "When anybody gets up a project and works the way Street has and sells it, I think that he is entitled to the fee or commission as well as a fellow that sells it after it is started. Anybody that comes in like a man and works as he has done, I think he is entitled to something for it."

When Camden County's Prosecuting Attorney Morgan Moulder took the stand, he answered this way when Rassieur asked if the residents of the county were for or against the dam: "Taking the county as a whole . . . I think the people are asking for a fair deal in the transactions and the condemnation of their property . . . I do not believe they are opposed to the proposition of its being built, but they ask, I think, that they would like to have a bridge across the lake . . . and they would like to have just compensation for the county property . . . aside from that, I think there are no objections."

Moulder went on to say, "They also take the attitude that it is futile for the people to oppose the project and for that reason if they are going to construct the dam we would like to have it done as quickly as possible than to retard business as they have the past few years."

Moulder and Sid Roach then engaged in a disagreement about whether Roach and Charles Morrow was contracted by the Camden County Court to oppose the dam in the hearing..

"Not to my knowledge," Moulder stated.

"Do you know that Judge Leonard Franklin of the county court authorized me to come in and answer for them on this?" Roach asked.

"I do not," from Moulder.

"They didn't tell you they *didn't* do it, did they?" Roach asked.

"No."

Roach told the commissioners, "I want to say this witness is in error that they are all in favor of it—the house is full of people that are opposed to it . . . when he stated that no one was opposed down there, he is not telling the truth."

Moulder: "There are many people that are opposed to it."

Roach: "The sentiment is very well divided?"

Moulder: "I think the majority are in favor of the dam."

Roach: "Under certain restrictions and conditions?"

Moulder: "Certainly."

Roach: "And without the restrictions and conditions they are opposed to it?

Moulder: "Yes."

Roach: "There is no suitable location for a courthouse for Linn Creek if the county seat was removed from the present site and the location would require the relocation at some point distant from the present location?"

Moulder: "I presume it might . . . but that is for the people to determine."

Roach: "Couldn't you make a guess just like you have been guessing on other things?"

Moulder: "I do not guess."

Ralph Street took the stand and told the commission all the steps he had taken and all the obstructions that had occurred in the six years since he had stepped off the train that cold February day in Bagnell to find a site for the dam he had dreamed of.

"I brought the project up to the point where we could have started construction in the fall of 1925 if the financial plans we had then had not fallen through," he said.

The Public Service Commissioners continued the hearing until July 5.

By the July meeting the matter of building a huge dam on the Osage River close to Bagnell, Missouri, had pretty much been decided. Stone & Webster, the country's largest hydro-electric builder, and the holding company Dillon, Read and Company had invested time and money studying the project and making preliminary engineering changes to adapt the dam to the needs of potential customer, Union Electric. A contract, perhaps, as Egan had said, the largest for electrical power to date in the country, was in the works for Union Electric to furnish power to the lead mines in southeastern Missouri. In trying financial times as existed then, and especially those to come, the mines were a very important industry in the state.

Nevertheless, the hardcore resistance in Linn Creek was not about to surrender their homes or their town and way of living to benefit industry in another part of the state. J.W. Vincent, the *Reveille* publisher in that town, and John Farmer, the banker and part owner in the suspension bridge across the Osage in Linn Creek, came prepared to have their say.

Mr. Rassieur, attorney for Union Electric, asked Vincent, "I was told that you were in favor of the project until Mr. Street refused to buy your newspaper—is that a fact?"

Vincent: "You're altogether mistaken."

Rassieur: "You wanted $6000 ($72,720) for the newspaper and he wouldn't pay that."

Vincent: "I never offered to sell my newspaper."

John Farmer who lived on nearby College Hill was asked if he thought there would be room for the town to be moved up there and for the courthouse and jail.

"I guess it could be made possible if you could get enough steam shovels and powder to blow the hill off and make a level spot for it.'

Theo Rassieur, Union Electric's attorney, and Julius Muench for the city of St. Louis, spent most of their questions on compensation due Ralph Street and Walter Cravens. Cravens was claiming he was owed between $360,000 ($4,392,000) and $420,000 ($5,124,000) for the money he put into the hydroelectric project out of his pocket and for promoting the dam and getting it started. Street, on the other hand, asked for $200,000 ($2,440,000) for his effort in launching the dam project. Street had a fair-sounding claim, considering he had discarded his law practice and devoted all of his time for almost five years on the dam with little compensation.

Muench showed interest in the Farmers Fund which Cravens had created. Here is how Ralph Street attempted to explain the connection of the Farmers Fund with the Kansas City Joint-Stock Land Bank and the Missouri Hydro-Electric Company:

JULIUS T. MUENCH: What is the Farmers Fund?

RALPH STREET: The company Mr. Cravens controlled.

MR. MUENCH: Did he buy the land for this project in the name of the Farmers Fund?

MR. STREET: No, sir.

MR. MUENCH: Well, for what purpose did he buy land in the name of the Farmers Fund?

MR. STREET: He traded some land the Land Bank had foreclosed and which he used the Farmers Fund as the nominee to carry the titles in the project area.

MR. MUENCH: Was the Farmers Fund used as the nominee for the Hydro-Electric company or the nominee for the Kansas City Joint-Stock Land Bank?

MR. STREET: For the Kansas City Joint-Stock Land Bank.

MR. MUENCH: He used the funds of the Kansas City Joint-Stock Land Bank to buy land which he took in the name of the Farmers Fund?

MR. STREET: No, this is what took place. The Land Bank, from time to time, had foreclosed on some farms and they put the titles to the farms that were foreclosed to the Farmers Fund.

MR. MUENCH: Did they buy any land?

MR. STREET: They foreclosed it and sold it to the Farmers Fund and they have traded that land for land down here along the river. The Hydro-Electric had nothing to do with these operations.

Street continued to try and distance himself from the Farmers Fund and the land trading that Cravens, the Farmers Fund and the Kansas City Joint-Stock Land bank were engaging in. He said when asked when the Farmers Fund was organized, "I would not be sure, but I think it was along in 22 or 23." Court records, however, show that the company was organized in 1925 with Cravens having 998 shares of capital stock, Alice B. Todd one share and Ralph Street one share. Those three made up the board of directors. Street said he had been a director but that he resigned after a "year or two."

When Muench asked if the original scheme had been to buy up all the land at the edge of the lake and sell or lease it for cottages and resorts, Street said, "No, . . . it developed we had to option the entire farm and we would have this excess land and we began to get inquiries about it and the idea grew that there would probably be a market for it by people who wanted to put cottages on the lake."

But, Street stressed that, while there was ridge land that would have ended up as shoreline in the options the Hydro-Electric Company had purchased for $5.00 each, none of the options ever resulted in land acquired by the company and all the options had expired.

Federal District Court Judge Merrill Otis announced on July 18 that Walter Cravens' hearing on a writ of habeas corpus was complete and would be ruled on soon.

On July 27, the Public Service Commission released an order granting Union Electric the right to acquire the assets of the Missouri Hydro-Electric Power Company for $766,959.27 ($9,356,903.09) and interest from May 31, 1929, and to the payment of $200,000 to Ralph Street for his effort in getting the dam started.

When Camden County's Prosecuting Attorney Morgan Moulder received the order, he answered the commission, saying:

"Camden County, by its Prosecuting Attorney, does hereby admit service on this day of a certified copy of an order of the Public Service Commission of Missouri, dated July 27, 1929, relative to case No. 6474, the terms and provisions of said order are not accepted and will not be obeyed and are protested against for the reasons appearing in the motion for a rehearing this day filed with the Public Service Commission."

Morgan Moulder,
Prosecuting Attorney for Camden County.

On July 31, the Federal Power Commission granted the change of license for the dam from the Missouri Hydro-Electric Power Company to Union Electric.

Plans for the dam reached a new phase on August 2 when the Union Electric Company announced it had purchased 20,000 acres of land from the Kansas City Joint Stock Land Bank. An agreement between Herman Langworthy, receiver for the bank, and Louis Egan, president of Union Electric Light and Power Company, submitted to the Farm Loan Board in Washington was approved.

J.W. Vincent, John Farmer and other citizens and taxpayers of Camden County filed an application for a rehearing on the commission's order August 2.

The Board of Trustees of the Village of Linn Creek met and approved Ordinance No. 46 employing Morgan Moulder, "to protect the interests of the aforesaid village in regard to damages which result from the proposed dam across the Osage River at Bagnell, Missouri. It is further agreed that the Village of Linn Creek, Missouri shall pay to Morgan M. Moulder as full and complete compensation for obtaining any award of commissioners or judgment in court 25 percent of all sums collected as compensation or damages to the village, and if any trial in any Circuit Court is necessary the additional sum of $25, as an appearance fee, and one-third of all sums collected in excess of the highest bona fide offer made prior to beginning of said suit in the circuit court."

Approving the ordinance were Myrtle Ayres, Myrtle Foster, Julia King and Sydney Moore. (Following the adoption of Constitutional Amendment 19, allowing women to vote, the citizens of Linn Creek had elected every woman on the ballot. Thus, the three women on the town council. They appointed the only man on the council as the town mayor.)

Union Electric President Louis Egan's letter to Missouri Governor Henry S. Caulfield, dated August 5, 1929, described the land purchase by Union Electric:

Dear Governor Caulfield:

> I know you will be interested to hear that Union Electric Light and Power Company on last Friday and Saturday took over the property of the Missouri Hydro-Electric Power Company. . . .
>
> Coincident with taking over the property of the Missouri Hydro-Electric Power Company we made a contract with the receiver of the Federal Joint Stock Land Bank at Kansas City for the purchase of approximately 20,000 acres of land located in the reservoir above Bagnell. It was necessary to have this contract approved by the Federal Farm Loan Board at Washington, which was done.

With these preliminaries out of the way we are executing our contract with Stone & Webster Engineering Corporation. They have about twenty engineers at Bagnell now and many more are on their way to join the organization. The construction of the railroad from Bagnell to the dam has been started; the Missouri Pacific branch line from Jefferson City to Bagnell is being strengthened; telephone lines from Jefferson City are being reconstructed; the campsite has been selected and from now on the work will proceed rapidly.

I am writing this letter to you because I know that you appreciate the importance of this piece of construction to the state of Missouri. It is one of the largest enterprises of its kind that has been undertaken in this country.

With my kindest regards to you,
Sincerely yours,
Louis H. Egan
President

In District Court, the Missouri Hydro-Electric Power Company, still under Cravens' control, impounded a half million dollars of funds received from Union Electric saying it was on the books as a credit to Cravens. The land bank said no, and claimed the money as part of those assets that belonged to the bank. The Hydro Company filed suit against the Land Bank in Federal Court, case number 1365. The court docket was weighted down with Cravens related litigation.. The following are the cases Judge Albert Reeves and the court had to get through before allocation of the all-of-a-sudden influx of cash from the Union Electric Company was finally decided:

#1259, H.M. Langworthy, receiver, Kansas City Joint Stock Land Bank vs Walter Cravens, Alice B. Todd, Kansas City Finance Company and Henry L. Jost, receiver, Missouri-Kansas Farms Company, for various sums owed the bank. American Surety Company, intervener, claim against Land Bank of $20,000.

#1362, Shouse, Doolittle & Morelock vs Land Bank for $7777.90 for services to the bank..

#921, Missouri-Kansas Farms Company vs Land Bank, for $655,611.57 and $73,461.66 by way of assignment to Walter Cravens.

#821, Land Bank vs Farmers Fund for all the assets and properties of Farmers Fund.

#822, Land Bank vs Kansas City Finance, Cravens, Todd and Street for $181,736.20; counter claim against Land Bank for $131,365.38.

#878, Cravens Mortgage Company vs Land Bank for $344,177.99 for commissions and expenses.

#370, Land Bank vs Hydro Company, Walter Cravens and M.M. Miller for 640 acres in Carter and Ripley Counties.

#1542, Land Bank vs Walter Cravens, Frank Harrison, F.H. Cary, J.B. Dillingham and M.M. Miller for house and lot in Linn Creek. Intervener Exchange Bank of Platte City, Missouri, for $2000 note on house and lot in Linn Creek.

#7352, Land Bank vs Alice B. Todd and American Surety Company for $20,000 surety bond on Alice B,.Todd.

#1231, Land Bank vs Walter Cravens to cancel one note, renewal note and recover 423 shares of stock of Safe Deposit Company of Kansas City, Missouri.

#293,409 (Circuit Court of Jackson County, Missouri), Kansas City Finance Company vs Safe Deposit Company for $2,680.94.

#1403, W.S. McLucas (representing Land Bank stockholders) vs Land Bank (bondholders), relief from statutory liabilities.

#71, Guy Huston Company Trustee vs Land Bank for $44,680.96 for commissions on sale of Land Bank farm loan bonds.

CONSTRUCTION BEGINS

PERMIT GRANTED TO BUILD BAGNELL DAM, read the headline in the July 27, 1929 edition of the *Eldon Advertiser*. "One hundred and eighty men will be put to work the first of the week," the paper went on. This notice appeared in the same issue to all the homeowners and businesses of the town:

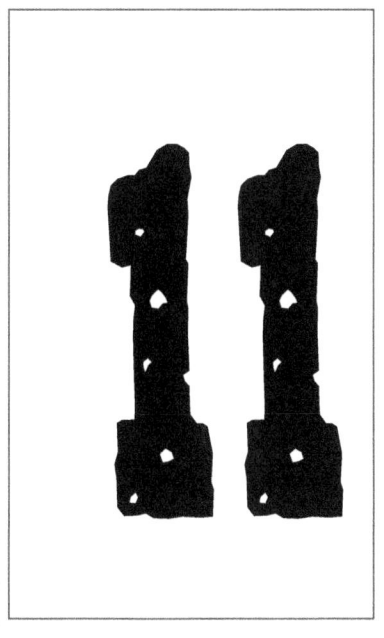

NOTICE!
Citizens of Eldon

We have been asked by the chief engineer of the Dam to make a list of every available house and room in Eldon and have it ready by Monday, July 29. Every public spirited citizen should try and make arrangements, if possible at all, to rent at least one room to these gentlemen.

Union Electric records show the following:

August 6, 1929 — Job started - General Clearing

One of the first orders of business for the new construction crews was to finish the railroad bridge across the river so that materials, men and equipment could be transported to the west side. A note here, the Osage ran from northwest to southeast at the point where the dam was to be constructed. Some of the references used north and south, some used east and west. On the east (north) side of the river were the bluffs that rose several hundred feet above the river level. At the top of the bluffs were the improvements Street had completed before all the construction stopped in December, 1925. The hilltop construction and the railroad that had been completed prior to the "official" start date of dam construction was described by Ralph Street during the Public Service Hearing on July 5, 1929:

> MR. CONRAD: Where is this railroad that you built?
>
> MR. STREET: It connects with the Missouri Pacific railroad at Bagnell and it was fully planned to extend it to the river and the dam site.
>
> MR. CONRAD: Are there any ties and rails laid?
>
> MR. STREET: The embankments are in there and the bridges and culverts are in and the rails are laid for a mile and a half or two miles and the ties were originally distributed the full distance, but a part of them were carried away in the floods.
>
> MR. CONRAD: How many bridges are there?
>
> MR. STREET: There is one over Little Gravois Creek at Bagnell that cost $15,000 ($182,250) and two or three other bridges over streams a hundred feet or more in distances and numerous culverts.
>
> MR. CONRAD: The railroad has never been operated?
>
> MR. STREET: No, sir.
>
> MR. CONRAD: Is that railroad embankment still in condition to be used?
>
> MR. STREET: Yes.
>
> MR. CONRAD: Is it solid and ready to have the ties and rails laid on it?
>
> MR. STREET: It is in excellent condition. The reason we discontinued work on it at the time was that it was soft and we could not operate a train and move the rails over it, but it has settled and is in an excellent condition now.

MR. CONRAD: And the rails—about a mile and a half laid, is that close to Bagnell or at the dam site?

MR. STREET: That is closest to Bagnell.

MR. CONRAD: How may bridges, or did you say there was only one constructed?

MR. STREET: Every bridge is constructed, all the culverts are in and the embankment built.

MR. CONRAD: How many bridges are there?

MR. STREET: There is this hundred foot steel suspension bridge at Bagnell and three others.

It was, in fact, November 21 of that year before the first steel was set on the Osage River Bridge. Concerning the other construction prior to the Union Electric takeover, Street said that at one time there were as many as 365 workers on the site. These expenditures by Street and Cravens on the constructions were listed for the Public Service Commission Hearing on July 27, 1929:

Surveys	$40,436.90 ($491,308.36)
Option Work	40,449.90 ($491,466.29)
Camp Equipment & Maintenance	215,746.63 ($2,621,321.55)
Engineering	56,569.55 ($687,320.03)
Core Drilling	22,451.75 ($272,788.76)
Construction Equipment	52,476.32 ($637,587.29)
Railroad bridges and Highway	55,232.05 ($671,069.41)
Truck rental	800.53 ($9726.44)
Logging	15,256.06 ($185,361.13)
Legal	14,827.87 ($180,158.62)
Administrative and Miscellaneous	118,244.52 ($1,436,670.92)
Interest during construction, paid and accrued to May 31,1929	108,425.62 ($1,317,371.28)
TOTAL	$766,959.27 ($9,318,555.13)

Here's how Street summed up the construction to that point to the commissioners at the Public Service Commission Hearing that year:

> "We built a highway from Number 54 at Bagnell and started the railroad and we built a bridge over a little creek connected with the Missouri Pacific Railroad and built waterworks, a sewage system at the dam site and built an administration building, and built two good-sized houses for housing the executives and the personnel and we started a temporary power house and mess hall, four bunk houses for the laborers and employees there, and had other work along that line outlined."

The highway, actually a gravel road from Bagnell, forked with one branch going to the upper camp on top of the eastern bluffs and the other branch going to the lower camp down in the flood land of the river. Donald Fitch described the work done there as having, "cleared the dam site and done all the engineering work in that connection."

Fitch said the reservoir area was, "17,000 acres of tillable land with the rest lying along the bluffs of the Osage River and for the most part it was rough, rocky land covered with timber and brush."

Walter Cravens did a poor job of describing the hydroelectric project on the Osage River to the jury when he and Miss Todd were in court in 1928:

> "The project was the building of a dam on the Osage River about three miles from Bagnell, Missouri. The dam was to be about 160 feet high and about 126 feet in length and I think 140 feet wide at the base and about 30 feet wide at the top. It was a reservoir proposition as the engineers had outlined it, and it was to produce from 75 to 100 thousand horsepower, which at that time was to be brought to Kansas City. There were various estimates as to its cost. I think a conservative estimate of the cost by the folks in Washington was about five million dollars."

The dam had grown since Ralph Street first envisioned it as a sixty foot high structure creating a lake no more than forty miles in length. The redesign that Stone & Webster did to enable Union Electric to meet the demands of the city of St. Louis as well as the St. Joseph Lead Company in Southeast Missouri was considerably grander, 2543 feet in length, 148 feet in height, 132 feet in width at spillway. The engineering plan that the Charles B. Hawley firm laid out was for an estimated $12,000,000 ($145,800,000). Stone & Webster was projecting a cost closer to $35,000,000 ($425,250,000). The project started out on a cost plus basis, so a final and firm price could not be established until the project was complete.

RAILROAD TRACKS BEING LAID FROM BAGNELL TO DAM SITE

The organization chart for the construction project as shown by Union Electric had Ole Davidson as the superintendent of the reservoir and H.C. Peeples as assistant superintendent. Stone & Webster's man, George P. Jessup was superintendent of construction. Jessup was fresh from his term as an officer on the Baker River Project for the Puget Sound Power and Light Company in Washington. Somewhat of a character, Jessup was a mechanical engineering graduate of Cornell University. He was known for wearing a white hat and for keeping an eye on the work site by telescope from his front porch atop the eastern river bluff. Jessup would charge down the bluff to accost and admonish any malingerer he might spot through the glass. Walter Malloy, a

GEORGE P. JESSUP, SUPERINTENDENT OF CONSTRUCTION FOR STONE & WEBSTER

resident accountant for Stone & Webster on the Osage River Project as it was called by the engineering firm, had this to say about Jessup:

"Maybe one of the most talented superintendents Stone & Webster ever had. He was a noted authority on hydro plants... A great organizer, he established a feeling all down the line with laborers, electricians, carpenters and everyone. They all had great respect for him."

Construction of a dam required it to be dewatered for final geological inspection, foundation improvement and the first stage of actual construction. For Bagnell Dam, a series of cofferdams were required. But, prior to the start of cofferdam construction, the construction site had to be cleared. Surveyors and logging crews were spread along the entire length of the planned reservoir to mark the elevations from 628 feet to 660 feet. That area had to be cleared of trees and structures with all brush, timber, rubbish and loose material burned or otherwise disposed of outside the submerged area. All of the 60,000 acres of lake area had to be marked and all of the 30,000 acres of the reservoir cleared.

Instructions for surveyors for dealing with belligerent landowners were not to go on the land. These instructions were not always followed. The surveyors and loggers were independent contractors operating under rules established by Union Electric.

On August 17, clearing started on the west side of the river. A few days later, an observation platform was built to allow onlookers to follow the construction from the east side.

Two thousand visitors to the observation platform were recorded on the last Sunday of October of that year.

Work continued on the hilltop for an enlargement of the mess hall, building the hospital and a jail for the use of the project's own police force. Living quarters would make up the majority of work expended on the east side prior to actual dam construction. Those facilities consisted of the large barracks for the laborers, individual houses for executives—three-room cottages and five room cottages—and an administration building.

CLEARING ON THE WEST SIDE OF THE RIVER, ACROSS FROM THE DAM SITE BEFORE THE START OF CONSTRUCTION

The Camden County Court was busy following the announcement of the beginning of construction on the dam. On that day, August 6, 1929, the Court issued an order that it would neither promote nor resist the building of the dam and that it would only do those acts that would protect county property in every way.

Several days later the court issued an order to Morgan Moulder, the prosecuting attorney, to withdraw the protest he had filed with the Public Service Commission on behalf of the county and filed a Withdrawal of Request with the Commission on August 8. On August 9, the Commission issued an order overruling the motion for a rehearing.

Moulder sent his own letter to the Commission on September 4 saying the following:

> I presume that you have my complaint of remonstrance on file, the complaint which I filed in behalf of Camden County. I think that Mr. Williams (attorney hired by the county) and the County Court of Camden County did withdraw my remonstrance, but the commission had no authority to discard my remonstrance upon the written request of the County Court and Roy D. Williams. As the legal representative of this county and as prosecuting attorney I filed the complaint to the order made by the commission and no person could withdraw that complaint except the prosecuting attorney of Camden County. It would be just as reasonable for the County Court to withdraw other legal instruments which I may file in the criminal courts and civil courts in behalf of my county which I legally represent and have exclusive authority to represent.
>
> If the aforesaid remonstrance has been destroyed I shall send you the copy, which I retained, and which was approved by the County Court and duly certified as being approved.
>
> In regard to the complaint filed by the village of Linn Creek, I shall be forced to appeal the case.
>
> Very sincerely,
> MORGAN M. MOULDER

Moulder followed through on his statement of appealing the case when he filed with the Circuit Court on September 22 for a per-

petual injunction against Union Electric and Stone and Webster to bar construction of the Bagnell Dam on the grounds of:
- The lake would inundate forty thousand acres of fertile land and destroy 200 miles of county roads
- The lake would divide the county into three separate parts without adequate means of crossing the water barrier
- The dam and the hydroelectric development were neither necessary nor convenient
- Neither the Public Service Commission nor the Federal Power Commission had the authority to give permission to block the navigable Osage River, that power being vested in Congress and the Legislature
- Due notice was not given as required
- Construction would obstruct and prevent navigation of the Osage River
- Construction of the dam would violate state law prohibiting removal of any county seat except by vote of two-thirds majority in a general election
- It would deprive the county of two-thirds of its revenue
- It would cause unwholesome and unhealthy conditions
- No provision is made for locks and chutes
- The reservoir would destroy and obstruct the use of several school buildings and destroy the source of maintenance

Moulder also filed a petition by 62 taxpaying citizens asking the court to set aside a purported contract between the county court and the Missouri Hydro Electric Power Company since transferred to Union Electric Light and Power Company agreeing to sell the courthouse, jail, etc. as without just consideration of due regard for the best interests of Camden County and not carried out in good faith according to its terms.

The Federal Power Commission amended the permit for Union Electric to build the Bagnell Dam on September 6, 1929, changing the date of completion to June 30, 1932 and adding the requirement to distribute oil or diluted Paris Green powder in shallow upper reaches of the reservoir to prevent the propagation of mosquitoes.

On October 9, 1929, the Massachusetts State Attorney filed a motion with the United States District Court in that state to strike the pleas of abatement filed there by defendants Guy Huston, Walter Cravens and five others.

The August 29 edition of the *Eldon Advertiser* said that 800 people were at that time working at the dam. The Story of Bagnell Dam, compiled and written by Carole Tellman Pilkington, stated that, "Every day several hundred more men would arrive, hopeful of finding work. They came by car, by rail, by bus and by foot. Most came without their families, but some did bring wives and children with them.

"People were everywhere, say those who remember the Dam building days. There were fields and fields of tents and shacks. People slept in cars, anywhere they could find a place. Tent camps sprang up. There were three, Dam Site, Spring Camp and Conner's Camp."

Six schools in the area were suddenly overcrowded and without adequate funds to provide for all of the new students. The Walnut Grove, Cooper, Pleasant Grove and Bowlin schools as well as Bagnell's elementary and high schools felt the rapid expansion of the student bodies. The state of Missouri increased their funding to the Bagnell schools by $390 ($4739) and to the Pleasant Grove school by $375 ($4556).

The pay for the laborers on the project ranged from 35 cents an hour to $1.25 an hour depending on the workman's skills. Steam operated digging equipment fueled by wood, coal or oil, was employed along with draglines and the pulling power of horses and mules, but the majority of the hard work of moving soil and building forms was done at 35 cents an hour. On October 29, 1929, the New York Stock Market suffered a collapse that officially kicked off the Great Depression. Most of the country was already in financial decline and the job market had shrunk dramatically. Locally, jobs were growing more scarce and the dam construction project offered jobs that had not existed before.

Lloyd Stone, uncle of Alan Sullivan, a consulting engineer for Ameren UE, told in an interview featured on the Bagnell Dam Documentary for the Dam's 75th anniversary, that he had heard about jobs at the construction site one Sunday night in church, so he and his dad and a neighbor went there the next day from their farm 12 miles from the site near Tuscumbia. They arrived there at six am.

"The line was so long you couldn't see the end of it," he said. When others began breaking the line instead of going to the end, a fight broke out. "My father and my neighbor just walked out of the line, but I was only 17 and I wanted a job."

One of the dam people saw them and offered the three of them a job.

"There was a lot of team (team of work horses) work there so I went home and got the team," he said.

Stone described the dam construction as, "the best thing that ever happened to Miller County."

The construction of the dam consisted of these major projects:

- West and east abutments—anchors, actually of the entire structure at each end
- The spillway section of 13 spillways through which the river would continue flowing downstream when the dam was completed
- The power station—the heart of the operation holding the six generators
- A diversion channel to route the river away from construction sites
- High voltage transmission lines to carry the power to St. Louis and to the Rivermines in Southeast Missouri
- Rerouting of U.S. Highway 54 atop the structure.

The two abutments, the spillway section and the power section would each need cofferdams around the sites that would drain the water from them and keep the river out while excavation took place down to the foundation dolomite sandstone rock.

On the last day of September, excavation began on the west abutment and the layout for the cofferdams at that abutment and for the spillway region. Steel-sheet piling was used to outline the cofferdams. Single lines of sheet piling were driven into the ground by six, steel-skid derricks. Dredges, clamshells, power shovels and three cubic yard and six cubic yard draglines completed excavation not done by horses and mules or by manual labor.

It was necessary to keep the river flowing through a diversion channel until it could be diverted through the notches and sluiceways of the spillway section.

By the end of 1929, excavation for both the east and west abutment was going on, cofferdams were under construction for the west abutment and the spillway section, the temporary power plant to provide 2500 watts of power was in operation and the 50,000 gallon water tank on top of the hill built by Pittsburgh Des Moines Steel Company was undergoing testing. Plus, the gravel plant at the Bagnell end of the newly constructed railroad from Bagnell to the dam site was being worked on.

Ralph Street now worked in the land acquisition office of Union Electric in Kansas City.

Walter Cravens was fighting removal to the United States District Court of Massachusetts to face trial after being indicted for illegally using the U.S. mail to sell falsely-labeled stock in his Kansas City Joint Stock Land Bank plus waiting for a decision of the Federal Appeals Court on his conviction and sentence of six years in prison.

Alice B. Todd was in Salina, Kansas with her relatives there, awaiting a year and a day in prison.

And a group of citizens in the town of Linn Creek was mounting a last, desperate effort to keep their town alive and stop the flooding of their valley.

WORK, WORK, WORK

BY THE BEGINNING of 1930, the workforce at the dam hovered at a thousand men. On the west side of the river, 4300 feet of railroad track had been laid with several hundred more feet added daily. Work had been suspended from December 24 through December 26 for the Christmas holiday. Trains were crossing the Osage River bridge daily, supplying materials and equipment to the west side for work preparing the abutment that would anchor the half-mile long dam at the western end.

Two huge air compressors were delivered December 30 following the pouring of their foundation a week earlier. The compressors were planned to be operational following the completion of the framing for their installation. The compressed air was intended to drive high-speed drills and air hammers needed for work in the rock.

A new 15-inch dredge was being assembled. An oil barge, steel barge and pontoons for the unit arrived up the river to the dam on Christmas day behind the towboat "Sterling." The Number One skid derrick had been moved to the east side to begin excavation for the spillway cofferdam to divert water away from the excavation necessary for building and pouring a foundation.

Ironically, one small steam driven generator in the powerhouse was operational, providing light for a portion of the camp busy building a hydroelectric plant. Two cars of fuel oil were received and unloaded. Two boilers were under pressure and a third to be completed in the next week.

Nearly 5000 acres of reservoir land was under contract to be cleared. Another 1000 men were employed on that project.

Cheers rang out in the five-room and three-room cottages on January 10, 1930, when the temporary power station was placed in service. Light bulbs glowed, radios blared and cottage occupants yelled and clapped when the power came on at supper time. Bad weather had reduced the workforce on January 11 to about 1500, 300

A SIX CUBIC YARD DRAGLINE (LEFT) AND A THREE-YARD DRAGLINE DID A MAJOR PORTION OF THE EXCAVATION. HERE THEY LOAD THE SOIL INTO RAIL CARS TO BE TRANSPORTED AWAY FROM THE SITE.

of them engaged in clearing the reservoir area. Bad weather slowed the axe chopping.

The W.E. Callahan Company was assembling their six-cubic-yard dragline that they expected to place in operation within the week, and also expected to have a three-cubic-yard dragline ready to begin excavation work on the spillway and the west abutment.

Piling was being driven into place for the trestle and tunnel for the sand and gravel storage plant. Four, two-cubic-yard tilting concrete mixers were placed on order. The planned output of the mixing plant when put into service would be 200 cubic yards of concrete per hour. Plans called for the plant to be electrically operated by 170 horsepower motors driven by 440 volts from the temporary power plant.

C.E. Wilson of Versailles was awarded the largest land-clearing contract to date for approximately 2000 acres along Gravois Creek.

January 7, 1930, Federal Judge Albert L. Reeves presided over a session held at the District Court of the United States for the Western Division of the Western District of Missouri, case number 1365, Missouri Hydro-Electric Power Company versus H.M. Langworthy, receiver of the Kansas City Joint Stock Land Bank. At this session, Henry Conrad spoke for the Hydro Company opposing Langworthy's attempt to force the Hydro company to tender to the court a $100,000 promotional fee included in Union Electric's payment to the Company. That $100,000, Conrad argued, was promised to Ralph Street by the Hydro-Company, Union Electric and the Missouri Public Service Commission. The money was half of what Street was supposed to receive for his promotion of the dam.

Cyrus Crane representing the land bank argued that Street, like Walter Cravens, had been an officer in both the Hydro Company and the land bank and as such was not entitled to any compensation other than salary from those two institutions.

"Further," he said, "by reason of the fact that funds, assets and properties of the said Land Bank were wrongfully diverted and used in the promotion and development of said water and power project . . . all the funds and profits realized from the development of said water and power project . . . belong to the Kansas City Joint Stock Land Bank and do not belong to said Street or to said Cravens or either of them."

In order to avoid a "multiplicity of suits," the $100,000 promised to Street should be tendered to the court for Judge Reeves to decide, Crane argued.

He asserted that when the Land Bank under Langworthy's leadership were arranging their accounting suit against Walter Cravens and other officers of the Land Bank, they had proposed to include the Hydro Company in the suits. Counsel for the Company urged them not to include the large payments of the bank in developing the dam in the suit against Cravens as they felt it might interfere with the completion of the sale of the option to Stone & Webster and Dillon, Read and Company.

"We didn't want to do that," Crane said, "so an arrangement was made with him (Mr. Street) . . . we would file this motion asking the court to determine whether or not that one hundred thousand dollars should be paid in determining the ownership . . ."

Conrad told the court he could not emphasize enough that "Under no circumstances, unless forced by the court, would we permit Mr. Street's rights to become embroiled in the controversy between the Land Bank and Mr. Cravens."

Conrad said he was, "insistent that this claim of Mr. Street stand on its own merits and not be engulfed in this unending litigation pending here between the Land Bank and Mr. Cravens."

Of Crane's charges of how the bank's money was falsely used to develop the dam, Conrad said, "If it happened, Mr. Street knew nothing about it. The money was coming from Cravens. Now Cravens was interested for the bank, not Street. Street was working for the Hydro.

"Here comes Street, working day and night—bulldog tenacity the unending determination that was evidenced by Mr. Street through those hours that were as black as any hours at Valley Forge were. This is an exceedingly small fee for the service rendered."

"This was 1927," Conrad told the court. "Here was the Hydro then upon the rocks. There were obligations outstanding of $250,000. Liens had been filed to the extent of seventy-five or a hundred thousand dollars. All this time the Land Bank sat still without a single assertion that it had any interest therein. It let the matter drop. It fastened the responsibility upon Street to wrestle with this matter.

"When they (the Land Bank and Receiver Langworthy) took the position they were going to claim the whole thing (the money paid by Union Electric) Mr. Street says, 'I am through. If you are going to get me in all these controversies between Cravens and the Bank, I will go no further.'"

But Conrad said that Street went before the Public Service Commission and after the two hearings in 1929, the Commission agreed the fee should be paid to Street.

Judge Reeves said he was not prepared to rule on the request of either party at the time, but asked for a summary from each.

On the evening of January 12, 1930, Jefferson City police found two girls, eight and nine years old, who they believed to be homeless and destitute. After buying them a hearty supper they turned the girls over to Captain Faubister of the Salvation Army. According to the Jefferson City *Post-Tribune*, the girls confessed they were planning a trip to Bagnell without telling their parents.

The temperature on January 18 hit a minus 25 degrees at Tuscumbia, Missouri.

The town of Bagnell looked back at the change from a year ago when most of the town's businessmen felt the town was dead, along with the dam project. January 1930, a very different town was alive. New buildings were going up and every building in town was occupied. Union Electric operated construction and material trains from the Missouri Pacific terminal in Bagnell to the dam. A year before, the only hotel in town had closed for lack of business. In January 1930, there were four or five larger hotels and rooming houses operating and practically every home kept roomers. There were grocery stores, meat markets, a drug store, a dime store, clothing stores, pool and billiard halls, barber shops, a steam laundry, used car lots and an electric lighting plant. Real estate values had greatly increased over a year ago.

None of the businesses had plans beyond the next two years for the time when the dam would be completed and the thousands of workers had moved on.

Routing for state highways was an ongoing subject of controversy. A Kansas City *Times* article on January 27, 1930, stated that a relocation plan for the highways in Camden County had been virtually agreed upon by county residents and the state highway commission. That would turn out to be far from the truth. Two proposals were under discussion, one requiring two bridges. One of the bridges would go across the Osage River near Hurricane Deck, the other across the Niangua River. This route would bring Highway 5 and Highway 54 together at a point about six miles south of the county seat of Linn Creek on a flat plateau which promoters and some residents thought would be the perfect place for a new county seat.

The power company, Union Electric, however, favored another route that would direct Route 5 southeast of Versailles to cross the completed Bagnell Dam and join Highway 54 about three miles from the town of Zebra. A new town being developed, Osage Beach, agreed to build a new schoolhouse and a new courthouse if that route was followed. The savings on that plan to the power company would be the cost of two bridges.

The highway commission said they lacked funds to build the two bridges. The commission interpreted the state law governing the location of the state highways to be in the hands of the commission. That interpretation did not sit well with residents of either Morgan County or Camden County as it would place the final word on the location of the new county seat in the hands of the state highway commission. One could almost see J.W. Vincent at his roll top desk in the *Reveille* office, red with apoplexy.

The workforce at the dam was in excess of 1500 as a break in the weather provided more allowable construction. A cut in the ice cleared a path for the 15 inch electric dredge to be moved to the east side of the river, placing it in service along with a ten inch dredge.

The Callahan Company placed their six cubic-yard dragline in operation and in conjunction with the three-cubic-yard dragline, some serious earth moving was going on.

A contract was awarded for a new bridge across Glaize Creek to replace the one in use that would be inundated.

The week ending February 1 saw continued excavation on the spillway section with both dredges and the six-cubic-yard dragline in operation. Two skid derricks worked day and night on closing the cofferdam there. The fifteen-inch electric dredge started excavation for the lower end of the channel that would divert the river from its bed to the spillway section, permitting the powerhouse cofferdam to be closed. Approximately 200,000 cubic yards would be excavated.

At the east abutment, two more skid derricks were driving steel sheeting for the cofferdam there. The work force at the dam was approximately 1275 men.

By the next week in February, earth excavation for the spillway section of the dam was complete. Work had started on a 12-foot wide trench into the rock at the face of the dam. A section of rock the full width of the dam and 200 feet long had been cleaned off. Rock excavation at the upper ends of both east and west abutments was complete and drilling and grouting operations were underway.

The four, two-yard concrete mixers were set into position and the batching equipment for measuring was being installed. Framing was taking place for the inclined belt conveyors that would transport the mixed concrete. The installation of gravel washing and screening equipment at the gravel plant was ongoing.

With the return of good weather, thirteen hundred men were now busy clearing land in the reservoir area.

Union Electric announced they had contracts to purchase over one-half of the needed acreage and that everything in the town of Linn Creek except for about 30 houses and stores had been bought. Notices of condemnation were filed against a number of owners who could not agree with the company on price.

One of the largest land purchase contracts was awarded to John

THE SPILLWAY COFFERDAM EXCAVATION INTO THE ROCK WALL ON THE EAST HILLSIDE AND THE FORMATION OF CONCRETE FORMS

S. McCrory, Linn Creek postmaster, his wife Maude and Thomas Ezard for three farms and a number of town lots in Linn Creek. The purchase price was $75,000 ($915,000).

Rain and melting ice drove the Osage River up 13 1/2 feet the next week, but did not hamper the workforce except for the dragline operations. But even with mud and high water, the six-cubic-yard and the three-cubic-yard machines were placed on 24 hour operation and moved about 4000 cubic yards of earth per day. The spillway cofferdam was closed February 7 and two derricks were digging material to fill the cells that enclosed it. The pumping operation waited on the necessary equipment. The two dredges were working on the diversion cut, the diesel unit at the upper end, the electric unit at the lower end. The concrete foundation for the concrete mixing plant was poured.

By mid-February the work force had grown to 2900 men with 1430 of them employed by subcontractors. A number of visitors toured the site including J.H. Manning, president, G.O. Muhlfield, chairman of the board, W.N. Patten, vice president and H.A. Hageman, chief hydraulic engineer, all from the Stone & Webster Engineering Company.

Six, 10-inch motor driven cofferdam pumps were installed in the spillway cut and by the end of the month the water level dropped to ten feet below the river level within the cofferdam. A three-cubic-yard dragline was placed in the bottom of the cofferdam. The W.E. Callahan Company now had three draglines excavating for the spillway and west abutment. The sand and gravel plant was nearing completion and power was being received from the temporary power plant. The framing for the cement mixing plant was nearing completion and the cement storage construction was started.

Equipment was moved into place to begin construction of the Grand Glaize Bridge near Zebra by the C.P. O'Reilly Company of St. Louis.

On February 21, 1930, the Committee on Banking and Currency of the Seventy-First Congress of the United States began a hearing on HR 9433, a bill to amend the Federal Farm Loan Act and other business. Louis McFadden of Pennsylvania was the chairman. Congressman Roy Fitzgerald of Ohio was the most outspoken witness before the committee. His great concern was with the stockholders of the joint stock land banks that had gone into receivership. The congressman admitted he was one of those stockholders.

The Great Depression was roaring throughout the land, especially in the Midwestern farming states. A drought brought diminished harvest return and many of the farms that had a mortgage did not make it through the harvest season. By the time the Committee began their hearing on the Farm Loan Act, three of the joint stock land banks in the U.S. had already gone into receivership including the Kansas City Joint Stock Land Bank under Walter Cravens.

Fitzgerald told the committee, "If that bank (the Kansas City Joint Stock Land Bank), with the permission and acquiescence of the

Farm Loan Board, had gone into a hydroelectric venture, much money would have been made. It was rumored that that was a highly profitable thing and would have worked out to the immense advantage of this bank. The board wavered. You cannot get aggressive action from persons upon who the great weight of bureaucratic responsibility is thrown. This occasion called for courage and some faith and apparently they got frightened and put a stop to this hydroelectric enterprise and apparently they lost faith in Walter Cravens and the men running the bank. They vacillated and brought this bank to failure."

Fitzgerald continued, "I am told they put this receivership in not because the bank was insolvent, but because they distrusted or disliked the president of the bank and they wanted to take control away from him."

To which Congressman F. Dickinson Letts of Iowa said, "I understood when the receiver took hold there was not enough money in the bank to pay interest."

Congressman Franklin Fort of New Jersey said, "They did not get him any too soon because this man was issuing notes to himself."

During the hearing the Farm Load Board proposed legislation to clarify the powers of the receivers under the Farm Loan Act, particularly with reference to the assessment of stockholders and their "double indemnity," clause of the existing law.

Fitzgerald said about the "double indemnity" clause where the stockholders lost their investment and then had to put an equal amount back into the bank, "If they put any more money in that stock, with its double liability, they are just sticking their fingers further into the trap."

The 71st Congress took no action on the matter. It was left to a later Congress in 1933 to pass an emergency farm loan act that would finally lead to liquidation of all the joint stock land banks.

An outbreak of spinal meningitis in the new housing developments between Bagnell and the job camp threatened to assume serious proportions when a child died from the disease at Dam Site and a few days later a man died from the same malady. Two other children were treated for meningitis in an isolated building within the Stone & Webster camp. One of the children did not survive.

Stone & Webster told a meeting of the State Board of Health physician, field inspector and the county health nurse that the company would furnish small, movable buildings to house and treat patients with contagious diseases. All employees at the dam were inoculated against smallpox and typhoid fever to preclude an epidemic among the rapidly growing population in the area. Miller County Court voted to make a substantial contribution towards the expenses of the State Health Department's work in connection with the new housing developments. State Health officials assigned full time to the development area were the health officer, a full time nurse and a health inspector.

A labor strike hit the dam site in early March in sympathy with union troubles elsewhere, but had subsided by the middle of the month and everyone was back to work. Callahan's three draglines moved 4200 cubic yards of earth per day cleaning the spillway section, then moved over to the west abutment area. The electric dredge completed all the excavation for the downstream end of the diversion channel and moved over to the east abutment cut. The diesel dredge moved from the diversion cut to the sand and gravel plant at Bagnell where it dug a basin for the new sand and gravel dredge made necessary by the low level of the river. All the excavating work at the dam was placed on a two-shift schedule.

Louis Egan, president of Union Electric, visited the site as did Ralph W. Street, now employed by the Union Electric Land and Development Company in Kansas City. Street the dreamer, seeing his long held dream materializing..

Twenty-five percent of the reservoir area was now cleared with over 1400 men engaged chopping trees and cleaning brush from the land.

Robert C. Williamson, employed by Stone & Webster and residing at Home Comfort Camp at Dam Site, reported his car stolen on March 23. Two workers at the dam engaged in an altercation in a Bagnell pool hall March 7. Their quarrel was over money and the quarrel led to Ben Butler bashing John Extend's skull with a stick of cordwood. Both were reported to have been drinking illegal alcohol. Extend was taken to the hospital in Jefferson City where it was thought he had a chance to survive the fracture in his head. Butler was arrested, but escaped and had not been seen since his sudden departure.

At the new observation platform erected for visitors to observe the construction progression, over 2000 people had been counted for each of the last two Sundays in March.

April 4 of that year, Attorney Theodore Rassieur and others representing Union Electric Light and Power Company appeared before the Camden County Court and presented a contract for the sale of the Camden County Courthouse, the courthouse square, jail, county roads and other county property. The offer for the courthouse was less than half of what the Missouri Hydro Electric Power Company had offered in 1926. The contract was not acted upon, but was placed with the county clerk for public inspection and further consideration.

April 9 saw the work crews at the dam begin pouring concrete for the piers of the construction bridge. This was the bridge that would be used to move equipment and materials into place for the construction of the dam. Pace of the work began to accelerate. On the 18th of the month, the steel sheet metal sheathing was set into place on the east side of the river for the upstream river cells. Pouring of concrete started on the 21st using a small mixer. The large mixer plant would not go into full operation until the 28th of the month. Two months later 100,000 yards of concrete had been poured.

During April, the work force at the dam went over 3000. Major accomplishments at the job during the month were progressing rapidly with the spring weather, but the most important milestone had been reached on the twenty-first of the month with the first concrete pouring at the west abutment for a foundation for that section of the dam and the highway bridge.

A progress report from the dam denied recent published reports about fatal accidents. A full time safety inspector was on the job at the site and both Union Electric and Stone & Webster insisted that safety work be an essential feature of the operation. A safety committee of foremen and workmen met weekly to make recommendations on job safety measures. A job hospital was maintained on the east side of the river and a first aid room with a nurse on the west side.

Judge A.L. Reeves listened to the pleas of the Camden County residents opposed to the construction of the dam on April 28 in the Federal District Court in Jefferson City. Charles M. Morrow and Sid C. Roach, St. Louis attorneys who had both lived in Linn Creek, represented the residents who came to the court asking for an injunction against continuing the dam construction.

The constitutionality of the Federal Water Power Act, under which a permit was issued for the dam, was attacked by the applicants for the injunction, on the theory that the State of Missouri owns all the waters within its boundaries and that one of the stipulations when Missouri was admitted to the Union was that its rivers would forever remain open highways. The dam, the suit claims, would hinder navigation. Other grounds offered for an injunction were that proper legal notice was not given, the dam would be a nuisance and a menace to health and that proper state consent was not given for taking of property.

Theodore Rassieur, chief counsel for the Union Electric Power and Light Company contended that all requirements of the water powers act had been met.

Judge Reeves said he would take the suit under advisement and render a decision as soon as possible.

Two towboats, the Sarah McDonald and the Sterling, were on the way upriver with four barges for handling the sand and gravel. Low water in the river hampered their progress. But rainfall in the Osage basin enabled a five foot rise by the first of May and the towboats completed their journey to Bagnell. Temporary power increased to 6000 kw when a second generator went into service. The first large pour of 3700 cubic yards of concrete from the main mixing plant was made on the first two days of May.

The spring weather contributed to a rosy outlook for the month.

144 DAM OVER TROUBLED WATERS

GENERAL VIEW OF CONSTRUCTION IN APRIL, 1930, LOOKING SOUTHWEST FROM EAST HILLSIDE. THIS IS THE VIEW GEORGE JESSUP HAD WHEN HE WATCHED FROM HIS PORCH FOR MALINGERERS.

The machine shop caught on fire and was lost to service. Concrete pouring went to 2000 cubic yards per day. The approaches to the Grand Glaize Bridge were being readied.

The Eldon *Advertiser* carried a regular column every week headed DAM GOSSIP. The May 15 issue had these juicy morsels:

> The Love Doctor says he can make it to Jefferson City in thirty minutes against the wind. K. D., you better wind up that Ingersoll next time!

> Mr. (Witches) Wiechers took in the windy corners of High Street Saturday afternoon. Also Andy and Joe Spinelli were admirers of Phoenix and Blue Moon.

> Ray Shimwell's chauffeur is fast improving in her driving, only the stops are more frequent.

Shocking news came from Bolivar, Missouri where Circuit Court Judge C.H. Skinker passed down a ruling on the case Camden County Prosecuting Attorney Morgan Moulder had filed in February to prevent the construction of Bagnell Dam. Judge Skinker ruled in favor of the county.

Union Electric, however, was not too concerned about what some county judge had ruled. They were doing all their legal battles through the federal court. They applied for a permit from the Public Service Commission on May 19, 1930, for the construction of transmission lines from Bagnell Dam to Rivermines in Flat River, Missouri and another to their Page Avenue plant in St. Louis. A hearing was held on June 11 and a certificate to construct two, three-phase, 132,000-volt lines to Southeast Missouri to the lead mines and two single circuit, three phase, 132,000-volt lines to the Page Avenue plant was granted. Union Electric stated that no consent, franchise or permit of any county, city, municipality or other public authority was necessary for authority to construct the transmission lines.

PROGRESS

WHEN CAMDEN COUNTY Presiding Judge Leonard Franklin signed a contract on behalf of the county to sell the courthouse and jail to the Missouri Hydro Electric Power Company in 1926, it was an illegal act, Missouri State Circuit Judge C.H. Skinker ruled on May 10, 1930. The judge said that the courthouse and jail could be abandoned and sold only with a two-thirds vote of the people. Further, he said the company's federal license did not include the authority of eminent domain that would enable it to condemn federal property.

Louis Egan, president of Union Electric made a trip to Linn Creek the next day, seeking a new contract from the Camden County Court. In view of Judge Skinker's ruling, the court was reluctant to enter into another contract. Morgan Moulder's suit in the federal court to halt production on the dam hung over the entire project.

The workers at the dam were undeterred. Another 18,300 cubic yards of concrete were poured. On May 16 a one-day pour of 3582 yards occurred. By May 22, concrete from five hoppers was being poured. Union Electric announced a log lodge was being constructed for executives just upstream from the Girl's Cottage. The name given to the lodge was Egan's Lodge.

Five-year-old Homer Earl Fields, son of Mr. and Mrs. Gaston M. Fields of Florence, Alabama, died after being struck by an automobile in Dam Site, according to the Eldon *Advertiser* on May 15.

THE CAMDEN COUNTY COURTHOUSE IN LINN CREEK THAT WAS PURCHASED BY UNION ELECTRIC BY CONDEMNATION FOR $30,000.

On January 16 of that year, 1930, Clint Webb had contracted to buy 160 acres of land then known as the Chipman farm from R.S. Doherty of Mystic, IA. For $2750 ($33,412.50). The farm was located at the exact point where highways 5 and 54 would, according to one set of the highway plans, intersect. Webb and his partner James Banner cleared the land and surveyed it into parcels.

In May, 1930, John T. Woodruff of Springfield, Missouri, became actively identified with the project and the development of a new town at the site. According to the Springfield *Daily News*, "After the surveys for the new routing of U.S. Highway 54 and State Highway 5 had been completed, the three men bought the large tract at the point where the two routes intersect, about two miles from the lake to be formed."

Banner and Webb held a barbecue at the site of the town they were building and invited the public for free food and drink. While there imbibing the handouts, county residents were shown a petition to name the bare spot in the pasture as the new county seat. According to one old timer who had attended as a youngster, the later in the day it got, the more willing people were to sign. The two developers were also offering buyers' a choice of lots in the yet-to-be-named town site.

The other towns in the county that J.W. Vincent had been convinced would never thresh it out among them as to which one would replace Linn Creek as the county seat, were ambushed by Webb and Banner. Vincent himself was originally convinced the town of Linn Creek would just move to higher ground near College Hill and the cemetery. He, in fact, moved printing equipment into his house there.

The Esthers, who owned the land upstream on Linn Creek, were encouraging residents to help form a new town there and many did. Linn Creek Postmaster John McCrory was among those who moved to that site, known at first as Estherville. Later, when a post office was started there in February 1931, McCrory registered the name of the town as Linn Creek, thus preserving the name of the original town.

Decateurville, Macks Creek and Climax Springs were caught off guard and never organized any real opposition to the new site.

On August 1, Banner and Webb presented a petition bearing signatures of more than 25 percent of the eligible voters in the county to the county court. The court set November 15 as the date to hold a public election on moving the county seat.

A school for children of parents living within the dam site itself, taught grades through the eighth and had room for 30 students. A bakeshop was open that could prepare 600 pies a day and 500 cakes.

The weekly report on the dam's progression was written in the Tuscumbia, Missouri, Miller County *Autogram* by a reporter to read like a soundbite the first week of June.

"The whirr of monster engines, the purr of locomotives, the cracking of gasoline engines, the popping of diesel engines, the grinding of huge carriers, the pounding of pile drivers, the barking of dinky engines, the bang of compressed air hammers, the whirring of the huge mixers, the swimming sound of the concrete as it glides down the chutes into the man-made cavern . . . the Osage River dam is taking place."

The reporter's description of the dam provided a close-up look at the activity there. He toured the mechanical plants where the electrical power was provided by two turbine generators sent up from Rivermines in Southeast Missouri. The lead mines there found them dispensable because when the big dam was completed, it would supply all the power needed at Rivermines. The boilers that provided the steam to drive the turbines came from Barberton, Ohio.

Next to the powerhouse was the air compressor room that provided high pressure air for drilling in the hard rock. The air was transported across the river in pipes. Adjacent to that room was the machine shop that caught fire earlier and was destroyed.

At the edge of the river sat the "dinky" ferry boat that seemed to be in constant operation delivering workers from one side to the other, powered by a gasoline engine driven drum and cable system. Soaring high overhead, the army of huge derricks unloaded coal, swung steel pilings into place, tugged dragline excavators or moved materials into the excavated portions of the dam. Great stacks of sheet pilings lay about, Y's, T's and right angles to form needed shapes in the cofferdams. The half-inch thick steel pilings were grooved at the edges to lock the sheets together to assemble the cofferdams.

Up flights of stairs one could stare down 75 feet into a large cavity where men scurried about performing various tasks. Huge floodlights were everywhere as the operation was now on a 24 hour a day schedule. Stone & Webster, by contract with the St. Joseph Lead Company, had to have at least two turbines operating by October 1 the next year, 1931. The goal of Stone & Webster at that particular time was to finish the spillway section by August 1. Then the river channel would be diverted through the spillway until the east end of the dam was completed.

The engineer showing the reporter through tells him, "We'd

like to see the river behave just as it has been doing until next June, then if it wants to rise, we'll have no objection for we must have a head of water before the turbines can be put to use."

Sucking type dredges on barges in the river were removing the silt on the west side of the river, approaching the dam from both sides. By August 1 when practically all of the excavating would be completed, the Osage would have a new channel through the spillway section where the concrete will have been completed up to the low-water level.

The reporter is told that the lower side of the dam would slope downstream from the top. The structure would be 130 feet thick at the bottom of the dam and 25 feet thick at the top. The bottom of the spillway section would incorporate a design to dissipate the enormous flow of water through the dam, permitting the water to flow harmlessly with no backwash

Looking down into the excavation inside the cofferdam, far below the level of the Osage, there was no water inside except around the edges where automatically operated pumps kept the cofferdam bottom dry. When the gravel and earth were removed by the huge draglines, a solid layer of limestone was exposed, just what was needed for a firm foundation for the massive dam. The limestone was found to be at least 200 feet thick by drilling through with diamond drills. All small cavities and shells were removed by pick and shovel and filled. An artesian well was found to be flowing through the bottom of the foundation. A pipe was inserted into the well and the water tested pure. Water from the well was used in the camp for the workers.

On the west side of the river, the monstrous six-yard dragline was being dismantled to be shipped to Arkansas for another job. Three trains were running from the concrete plant delivering fresh concrete to the bottom of the excavated cofferdam where large concrete piers were rising. On these piers, steel structures were being placed and the reporter was reminded of a tinker toy set boys played with.

The reporter admired the riggers as he watched them climb to the top of the 60-foot steel structures using only their hands and feet, gripping the grooves in the beams. These were the highest paid men because their work was so hazardous, requiring enormous levels of skill, nerve and strength.

At the great concrete mixing plant, conveyors brought in the sand, gravel, cement and water. All the sand and gravel was tested and weighed for the water it contained and the exact measure of water added to the mixture to ensure the proper consistency. The mixer plant consisted of four mixers, each having the capacity of two cubic yards of mixed concrete ready to pour.

Jutting from the mixing plant were four muzzles looking like cannons or mortars which dispatched the concrete into three dinky trains—the fourth to be added later—in pairs, two at a time into the car. The train moved forward and the other two muzzles dumped concrete into the next car on the train. The train moved out and another took its place. Everything moved with clockwork. The train delivered its contents to the site within the cofferdam, then took another track beneath the bridge running from the mixing plant and got back in line for another load of concrete.

Streams of concrete slid into place making pools inside forms where men in hip boots, knee deep in the concrete, shoveled it into the corners. Parts of the forms had been removed from one section, revealing a concrete wall almost to the level of the river. Some of the steel structure used to support the forms that created the concrete walls would be retained after the dam was finished. Other beams would be cut away with torches as the walls were finished.

Three hundred and thirty thousand cubic yards of earth had to be moved by August 1 in order to divert the river through the spillway. The river would be moved out of the way of the working men.

State School Superintendent Lee and County School Superintendent Snodgrass studied the situation in the Bagnell and Pleasant Grove School Districts where the enrollment there had increased from 75 to 100 students per year to over 500 due to the influx of workers at the dam, and recommended consolidation of the two districts in order that students have the opportunity for instruction.

On June 5, 24 year-old Howard Pierce fell to his death from the top of the bridge into the excavated spillway section 70 feet below. Pierce was one of two riggers who were swinging the concrete hopper into place when one side of the hopper broke loose and Pierce fell to his death. The other rigger managed to hold on. Pierce's fatality was the second at the dam site since August 1929. Pierce's brother, also working for Stone & Webster, was on the site when his brother died. They were from Iowa.

On June 6, a record of 4863 cubic yards of concrete was poured in a 24-hour period. By June 9, 102,480 cubic yards had been poured making up a fifth of the total that would be required for the dam. The total employment at the dam at that time was 3565 men, about 700 of them employed in reservoir clearing. Six large piers for the Grand Glaize Bridge were being poured and were attracting attention by travelers between Bagnell and Linn Creek.

The Osage Hotel and Ward Restaurant of Bagnell and the Day and Night Cafe in Dam Site were raided by Miller County Sheriff Charles Abbott, Prosecuting Attorney R. Feindorf and Chief Deputy H. J. Smith of the Stone & Webster camp. Six men and one woman were arrested for selling illegal alcoholic beverages.

Union Electric placed an order with Westinghouse Electric for the vertical water-wheel type generators to be installed in the dam. Ready to be shipped from Chattanooga, Tennessee, were the steel, penstock liners that direct the river's flow into the turbine generators.

Another record at the dam for concrete poured in a 24-hour period was set on June 10 when 5070 cubic yards was poured. A total of 30,000 cubic yards of concrete was poured for the week.

A man named Hugh D. Cooper claimed a better 24 hour record of poured concrete on a project in Russia, but engineers at the dam said Russia was a long ways off and they're not relinquishing their title until they've checked up a bit.

Surveyors were at work in Miller and Osage Counties locating the center of the transmission lines from the dam to St. Louis and from the dam to Rivermines. The line to St. Louis to Page Avenue was to be

138 miles and the line to Rivermines 122 miles. The lines, which would carry 132,000 volts, ran northeast of Bagnell and crossed the Miller County line into Osage County near Meta on H-type wooden poles for the line to St. Louis and on steel towers for the line to Rivermines. The line through Miller County crossed Highway 54 near the H.E. (Dunk) Howser farm on the Little Gravois Creek, through the flatwoods country to Hall's store on Highway 52.

Stone & Webster representatives were acquiring easements in Miller County for the lines. Sixty-two tracts of land in Miller County were involved. The right-of-way was 125 feet wide and settlement for the easement was at $350 per mile.

June 19 appeared to be doomsday for the town of Linn Creek. Federal Judge A.L. Reeves declined to issue an injunction against Union Electric as Morgan Moulder and a group of town residents had asked.

The petitioners had used as reason for the injunction the theory that the Osage River was an open highway by agreement at the time Missouri entered the Union. Judge Reeves said the evidence showed that the Osage and Niangua Rivers were classified as navigable streams and that in his opinion the dam, instead of impairing navigation, would improve it, deepening the channel above the dam and probably aiding shipping below, in that the waters would be released in a constant stream.

"I had to construe the federal water power act," the judge said, "and found it applicable in the case of the proposed dam."

Another argument in Moulder's case was that the property to be submerged was taken without due process of law. Judge Reeves ruled that the property could be taken by the proper action of indemnification under the right of eminent domain. Besides, he said, most of the property to be affected by the dam had already been purchased by the power company.

The suit also questioned whether land dedicated for public use such as the courthouse and the 24 schools to be inundated by the dam could be properly taken under the eminent domain law.

On the question of the sale of the courthouse square in Linn Creek that Judge Skinker of the Circuit Court had ruled on May 10 as being illegal, Judge Reeves passed on that question. "In effect," he said, "I simply decided that the power company could go ahead with its work on the dam."

Moulder and the other attorneys who brought the suit said they planned to take the case to the United States Supreme Court.

A rise in the river hampered work on the spillway during the week ending June 23. The concrete poured that week was 29,000 cubic feet. The project was ahead of schedule so that on June 24 the work schedule changed from three shifts per day to two. At 4:30 p.m on June 25, the placing of 100,000 cubic yards of concrete since June 1 was celebrated by placing a flag on top of the mixing plant and blowing simultaneous whistles on all the derricks. This was more concrete than had ever been poured from a single mixing plant in one month. The total concrete now in place was about one-third of the total that would be poured for the entire dam and powerhouse. The dredges and draglines were working on the diversion channel cut.

Word from the dam was that for the next ten or twelve weeks, concrete pouring would continue at a rate of 2000 cubic yards per day. All work was stopped at the dam from the evening of July 3 until the morning of July 7 when work was continued again, now on a two-per-day shift instead of three.

The steel sheeting on the upstream side of the west abutment was pulled and would be reused in the cofferdam for the power plant. Two of the three traveling gantrys on the construction bridge were in operation and assembly of the third was underway. Because of the re-arrangement of schedules, the work force at the dam was now about 2900 with 630 at work clearing the reservoir area and 70 at work on the Grand Glaize Bridge.

Construction on the $135,000,000 ($1,647,000,000) Boulder Canyon Dam in Nevada began on July 7.

United States Attorney General Mitchell ruled in a case affecting a power development in Kentucky that the federal power commission must act on a request by a power company to build a hydroelectric plant despite protests of those who want the site for a public park. The decision had interests in Camden County where Union Electric had started condemnation action against the Snyder heirs, owners of the famous scenic wonder Ha Ha Tonka, 12 miles south of Linn Creek,

On July 17, two big raids by law enforcement officers at Bagnell and Damsite resulted in the arrest of George Redden of the Joker Inn in Bagnell and George and Alice Storms at the Storms Hotel in Dam Site for selling illegal whiskey.

The State Health Department ordered Union Electric to remove all the bodies from the basin to be flooded. To get in touch with kinfolk of all the dead and to secure orders for their removal, the company began running ads in area newspapers asking people having deceased relatives buried in the flooded area of the Osage River development to contact them. They told those who desired to have the remains of relatives removed, arrangements would be made to remove them to a new cemetery in a sightly location outside the reservoir area and with provision for permanent care. The new graves were marked with indestructible markers. In case of unknown dead, photographs were taken of the graves and surroundings in the old cemetery and plats made showing exactly where each grave had been. A number was assigned in the new cemetery so that in later years. a relative of the dead could by study of the plats and photographs find the new grave.

A 50-foot channel was opened for passage of the river in the diversion cut during the last week of July 1930. Sheeting was being removed from the cofferdam in the spillway section to be re-used in the power station cofferdam. A 200-foot tower with a suspended one cubic yard bucket was under construction on the east side of the river. The bucket would be used to pour concrete for the east abutment and the highway approach.

According to the rainfall reports in Miller County, July 1930 was the driest July on record. The Missouri corn crop was expected to be fifty percent of normal or about 13.5 bushels per acre. July ended with 3170 men employed at the dam, 880 of them clearing land.

When the cofferdam for the diversion channel was closed, the river was so low that about three hours was required for the river to rise sufficiently to flow through the spillway notches and sluices. Concrete was being transferred to the bucket on the 200-foot tower and poured into chutes and into the east abutment area.

Morgan Moulder filed suit in state Circuit Court on August 11 asking for a temporary injunction against Union Electric and Stone & Webster from filing, instituting and prosecuting cause against Camden County to condemn and appropriate county real estate including the county courthouse and jail.

The county court's minutes on that date stated: "In the matter of Case Number 233: In equity in the Federal Court of the Central Division of Missouri-The State of Missouri and Camden County complaints against Union Electric Land and Development Company and Stone and Webster now pending in the United States District Court at Central Division of Western District of Missouri, order and direct Morgan Moulder to prepare, perfect and prosecute such appeal in cause as will best protect public interest of Camden County and the State of Missouri, to take all steps necessary to protect and prosecute such appeal to the Circuit Court of the Appeals and to the Supreme Court of the United States if that be necessary."

Case Number 233 was the case that combined a number of condemnation suits brought by Union Electric against individual landowners and against Camden County and the city of Linn Creek.

The Cook-O'Brien Company of Kansas City made a start on cutting a 60 foot deep cut on the Highway 54 approach at the east end of the dam. Earth excavation for the power house area was nearly complete on August 19 when a total of 3575 men were employed, 827 clearing the land, 165 employed on transmission line clearing. and 41 at the Grand Glaize Bridge. A portion of the Houston farm near Bagnell was used for a landing strip for Union Electric's tri-motor Ford aircraft.

The two draglines excavating the upstream diversion channel

completed their work on August 15. One dragline had been moved to the power station cofferdam, the other was backfilling at the west abutment.

Two sand rolls were now employed at the sand and gravel plant crushing 30 tons of gravel an hour that was one-half inch in size or less.

Concrete continued to be poured at the east and west abutments. Approximately 42 percent of the total concrete for the entire dam had been poured.

Waterwheel equipment being received was six draft tube liners, five penstocks and three spiral casings. Employment at the dam was 3250 men, 750 in land clearing, 120 on transmission lines and 55 at the Grand Glaize Bridge.

Ralph Street, now representing Union Electric Company, along with Ole Davidson, superintendent of dam construction, met with twenty citizens from the town of Brumley, located in eastern Miller County, to determine what action to take in settlement for roads that would be submerged by the lake formed by Bagnell dam. The company proposed re-locating the road and building a low water bridge across the Glaize Creek, but the increased length of the relocation was not agreeable to the farmers in attendance. Street pointed out that the company had already purchased most of the farms that would be affected.

The County Court of Camden County, Presiding Judge Leonard Franklin, Associate Judges Charles Green and C.M. Jarrett, along with the other elected county officials, Prosecuting Attorney Morgan Moulder, County Clerk Charles Huddleston and Circuit Clerk Frank Lewis, were notified to appear before Federal Judge Reeves in Kansas City August 27 on an application of the Union Electric Power Company for an order restraining the county against the company.

To which J.W. Vincent quoted from the St. Louis *Star*,

"Chief Justice Hughes, addressing the American Bar Association in Chicago, told the states to fight for their rights against federal encroachment for only by that method could the United States ecape a federal despotism.

"State sovereignty has seldom been more seriously or insidiously attacked than in Judge Reeves' action . . . forbidding state courts to protect state sovereignty over the Camden County courthouse and jail and authorizing a public utility company to condemn them for power purposes."

The residents of Linn Creek who were putting up a stiff resis-

THE CUT THROUGH THE EAST BLUFF PROVIDING ACCESS TO HIGHWAY 54 CROSSING ON TOP OF BAGNELL DAM

tance to the building of the dam received a "double whammy" in the last week of August. Federal District Court Judge Albert L. Reeves responded to a suit filed by Union Electric Light and Power and granted an injunction restraining Prosecuting Attorney Morgan Moulder, members of the Camden County Court and its attorneys from taking any further action in the state courts in connection with the construction of Bagnell Dam. The company filed a condemnation suit, condemning the Camden County courthouse, the jail and approximately 60 miles of county roads.

Fifty-six properties in the town of Linn Creek that had been purchased by Union Electric were ordered by the company to be vacated by September 1. The buildings affected included most of the businesses except for the Ayers and Seaton Service Station and the Moulder Hotel.

The Kansas City Joint Stock Land Bank was back in the news September 2 with plans to rescue the bank. The plans, presented by San Francisco financier A.O. Stewart, were conditioned on 95 percent of the bondholders in the bank turning the bonds in for 60 cents on the dollar or accepting new bonds pared down 15 percent. The stockholders ended up with nothing for their stock, but most of them favored the plan as it relieved them of the double liability of putting more money back into the bank. Bondholders were given until December 15 to choose which portion of the plan they would accept.

Back at the construction area, the cofferdam for the power station had been de-watered after 25,000 cubic yards of earth was removed and used to fill the cells making up the cofferdam. Material for the transmission lines were in place and digging of holes had been started. Four officials of the Union Electric Company, including President Louis Egan, flew into the new landing strip on the Houston farm and visited the dam construction.

On September 6, the first pour of concrete was made in the power station area. Steel girders for the highway construction over the dam were set in place and the forms for highway concrete were built. Concrete was poured in the east highway abutment. Foundations for the turbines were poured as well as the headworks and draft tubes started.

Also on September 6 the Camden County Court voted to go to court again, this time against the Missouri State Highway Commission. The commission had decided to end Highway 5 at the water's edge at Hurricane Deck. The lawsuit, filed in conjunction with Morgan County, would force the commission to reconsider and route the highway through Camden County and the location planned for the new Camden County seat to Laclede County. That would include new bridges across the Osage River near Hurricane Deck and across the Niangua River.

The commission's plan would reroute Highway 5 to merge with Highway 52 at Versailles connecting it with Highway 54 at Eldon and across the Bagnell Dam when completed. That would throw a great area of trade territory belonging to Kansas City to the eastern half of the state including St. Louis.

Louis Baker, editor and publisher of the *Versailles Statesman* implied favoritism toward St. Louis when he was outspoken about the commission members, especially Jesse McDonald of St. Louis:

"Judge McDonald's attitude toward road matters affecting Camden and Morgan Counties has been offensive and inconsiderate. His utterances would indicate a desire on his part to promote private interests, even to the extent of damaging a part of the state in which he lives."

The two counties retained L. Newton Wilder, former attorney for the State Highway Commission. In late October, Wilder announced plans to file the suit in the 14th District in Cole County.

On September 24, the work schedule at the dam went back to the three a day shift which resulted in setting a new one-day record two days later when 5082 cubic yards of concrete was poured, eclipsing the June 10 record of 5070 cubic yards. Sixty-five percent of all the concrete had now been poured. Concrete for about 900 feet of highway at the west end had been poured and steel for five bays for the highway and operating deck over the spillway section were placed. Steel conduit for the penstocks leading to the turbines were started for the eight units.

Union Electric started a regular schedule for airline travel from Lambert Field in St. Louis to the new airfield near Bagnell for employees and executives of the company. The work force at the dam site

MEMBERS OF THE AMERICAN SOCIETY OF CIVIL ENGINEERS TOURING BAGNELL DAM

was 3515 men.

On October 4, 600 members of the American Society of Civil Engineers who were in attendance at their annual meeting in St. Louis, made an inspection trip to Bagnell Dam. As guests of the railroad, they rode a special train to Bagnell where a special construction locomotive took the train to the construction site.

All foundation concrete for the dam and for the power station had been poured by the first week of October. By late October, 82 percent of the concrete had been poured at the dam. The penstock liners were erected and the service units had been concreted up to the intake. The number employed by the project was 4055.

Construction Chief George P. Jessup talked with the Stone & Webster employees of Warsaw and displayed pine models of different portions of the dam. Jessup gave a short description of the dam area they and Union Electric had prepared for the workers on the site. There were thirty, two-room cottages, forty, five-room cottages, and bunkhouses sufficient to take care of 5000 workmen. Jessup said that for a man to be a good worker he must have plenty to eat and a good place to sleep. The camp had a hospital with a capacity for 50 patients, four doctors and six nurses. Three first aid stations were scattered in the camp. Jessup said the temporary powerhouse generated more current than was used by the city of Jefferson City.

Cravens fortunes improved on October 27, 1930, when the U.S. Attorney in the United States District Court in Massachusetts filed an entry of Nolle Proseque to all defendants meaning he would no longer prosecute the case there against Cravens and Guy Huston among others.

As election day approached in Camden County, J.W. Vincent cautioned readers of the *Reveille*: "Further agitation of the matter can serve no useful purpose. Propaganda, for or against the proposition might inflame personal or sectional feeling and could certainly be of no benefit in arriving at a wise conclusion. The choice of the people should be entirely free and untrammeled."

When election day came, November 15, 1930, the voters of the county elected to move the county seat by a vote of 2487 to 473 against, the move even being approved by citizens of the old county seat of Linn Creek. With houses and businesses being burned, the trees cut to the ground and over half the residents moved out, those remaining saw that resistance was futile. The only hope left were the courts where Morgan Moulder had filed for an injunction that threatened to be overruled by the federal judge Albert Reeves. And for those who fought to the last gasp, there were the condemnation suits filed against them by Union Electric.

The first of two 70-ton gantry cranes was being assembled by mid November. Eighty-five percent of the total concrete had now been poured. DAM GOSSIP in the December 25 issue of the Eldon Advertiser:

> Miss Clara, speaking over the local telephone exchange, was telling of the many Christmas presents she has received. "My Mules have come." Now all she wants is a nice red wagon.

Billie Byrne, the Vagabond Lover, received a beautiful bright red necktie from one of his many lady admirers, with a note, "The Season's Greetings, with affection—Alice.

"Poor Boy" Martin of the hard pulling riggers, bought a 187-pound hog for his Christmas dinner, but he says it is tough going without a drop of "Christmas Spirits" in the house. Try a can of sterno, or a bottle of hair tonic.

The 1930 census showed an Alice B. Todd, born in Kansas, living in Minneapolis, Minnesota, as a lodger.

As 1930 drew to a close, work at the dam was started on the 80-ton reinforced concrete slabs that would be used for the final closure of the 10 by 15 foot sluiceways through which the river flowed. Ninety-one percent of the concrete, over one half million cubic yards, had been poured and the sand and gravel plant closed, there being enough material on hand to finish the job. Four of the six scroll cases were concreted into place in the waterwheel section of the power plant with number 6 started on December 22. The work of removing the cofferdam at the upstream side of the power plant was practically complete.

RISING WATERS

THE ROTOR for the Number One generating unit arrived on the fourth day of January 1931. Work continued on the sluice gates and the highway slab which was completed the last day of January. Union Electric officials denied reports that the highway across the dam would be opening before their announced date of June 1, 1931.

The Camden County Court met in the Linn Creek School building on January 6, the stone courthouse having been condemned.

Ralph Street, the dreamer, was now the goodwill ambassador for Union Electric. At the January, 1931, meeting of the Miller County Court, he handed over a check to the county from the company for $17,200. The county said the money would be used to build a new road near the Glaize Creek crossing on the Brumley-Linn Creek road. Union Electric had rejected the proposal to build a bridge across the creek for the farmers in the area because of the cost. The settlement for the new road was based on an estimate by the State Highway Department.

Ninety-five percent of the concrete had been poured by the end of January. All the scroll cases for the waterwheels were now encased in concrete, leaving only the walls and a part of the roof to be finished. The opening in the east abutment for railroad access was closed. The first 33,500 horsepower water wheel runner arrived at the dam and was installed along with the main shaft. The runner is the moving element rotated by falling water and in turn, through the main shaft, rotates the electric generator. Six generators would be installed, but there would be openings for two additional to be added later.

The two, 70 ton gate-handling gantry cranes were placed in operation. These cranes would be used to close the gates to the spillway and to the water wheels. The main 150-ton power crane that would be used to place the generators in place was erected. The first of eight 70 ton steel gates that would close the intakes to the water wheels was received.

The steel taintor gates weighing 27 tons each had been installed to the twelve spillway openings. Thirteen spillway openings had been poured, but the thirteenth was concreted shut. A myth was started that Union Electric officials felt superstitious about the thirteen gates. Stone & Webster said that twelve openings were adequate to meet any flood condition that had ever been recorded on the Osage.

A driver on his way to view the work on the new dam, described the drive across the new Grand Glaize Bridge as, "resting nearly 150 feet above the valley which will soon be buried under 100 feet of water from Lake Osage, the new bridge is impressive and rather breathtaking when you first venture out on it."

On February 2, closure of the notches in the spillway openings was begun. The flow of the river was now confined to the five sluiceways through the spillway. Word had already been sent out from Union Electric to all the residents still in the reservoir area 129 miles upstream on the Osage, "Clear out by February 1."

February 19, four pm, the first of five sluiceways was closed by the lowering of a 77-ton slab into place. By seven pm all five had been closed and the formation of a new lake, the largest ever formed by man to that date, now being designated Lake of the Ozarks, had begun. Just enough water was let through the sluice gates to water the livestock downstream and to float a ferry boat a mile away from the dam.

By 7 o'clock the following morning the new lake had risen nine feet and that morning the "bottom dropped out of the river," as the old timers in Tuscumbia put it, with the government's gauge of the level of the Osage downstream at Tuscumbia dropping to zero.

ON FEBRUARY 2, 1931, THE SPILLWAY NOTCHES WERE CLOSED LEAVING ONLY ONE OF THE FIVE SLUICEWAYS TO ALLOW FLOW DOWNSTREAM.

With work on the dam nearly complete, many resorts and private cabins were beginning to pop up along the banks of the lake-to-be. The thrown-together camps of the workers clearing the reservoir areas were falling down or being taken down.

The transmission line to St. Louis was completed across Miller County except for the river crossing at Marys Home, with poles set all the way to St. Louis. The steel towers going to Rivermines in Southeast Missouri were completed from the dam to Iberia.

A small water-driven service unit was placed into service on April 9, generating the first power produced by the harnessing of the Osage River. Although the unit produced less than one-tenth of the power that would come from just one of the six huge generators to be placed in service starting in July, this marked the date when water power began to take over at the dam.

Scroll cases for the water wheels were all encased in concrete by the end of January. Stator and rotor work continued through February.

The last cofferdam at the downstream service power station was pumped full of water to test for leaks. When the water was pumped out, the last of the cofferdams was taken down and the power station structure stood on the river floor in its final and permanent condition.

On March 6, 1931, a document titled Assessment of Settlement and Release and Stipulation and Dismissal was signed in Federal District Court by all the parties involved in the litigation Walter Cravens had saddled the various companies including the Land Bank and the Hydro Company with. Out of court settlements were agreed to and not made public in most of the cases. The convoluted schemes Cravens and Alice B. Todd had created in weaving the Land Bank's money through all of Cravens' various companies, resulted in an even more convoluted route for allocation of funds.

In case number 1365, of the total of $630,153.65 held in escrow from the Union Electric funds and contested in court, the attorneys headed by Henry Conrad and Henry Jost, receiver for Missouri-

RISING WATERS 169

LOOKING UPSTREAM JANUARY 31, 1931, BEFORE CLOSING SPILLWAY NOTCHES

LAKE OF THE OZARKS IS FORMING IN MARCH, 1931, AFTER THE CLOSING OF THE SPILLWAY NOTCHES IN FEBRUARY

Kansas Farms were awarded $575,000 to be distributed among the clients retaining them. The remainder of the impounded funds were turned over to Langworthy and the Land Bank. This was the case that decided how much Ralph Street got out of the dam, which is unsure, and the amount Cravens got which would forever remain in controversy.

One interesting ruling made by Judge Reeves was the cancellation of a contract among Missouri Hydro Power Company, Walter Cravens and Ralph Street that would have given Cravens and Street an option on all the land bordering the newly formed lake.

On March 7, a 12 inch snow fell on the area. On March 16, half the downtown of Bagnell burned and two men lost their lives. Fire departments came from Eldon and Jefferson City to help fight the fire. The bodies of Jesse Brown, a worker at the dam, from Ravenden Springs, Arkansas, and an unidentified man were found in the remains.

Miller County Sheriff Abbott and Deputies Smith and Sooter arrested a man for stealing shoes, seven men for engaging in a poker game for money and one man for possessing a full pint of liquor along the road between the Union Electric property and Dam Site. The man they apprehended after observing him trying to hide the shoes in leaves, as the Miller County *Autogram* put it, "showed a strong inclination to leave for other parts, but was halted and taken into custody."

The man with the stolen shoes—oddly enough, both for the same foot—and the seven gamblers paid fines of $50 plus costs while the man with the "full pint" had to shell out $200 to stay out of jail.

When Union Electric resorted to condemnation proceedings against Morgan County for the county roads and bridges damaged by the forming lake, the engineer that the county had employed—with agreement at the time of Union Electric—submitted a bill for $1200 to the county. The federal court appointed appraisers for the county properties and the power company paid $126,575 ($1,544,215) to the county. The county figured they were out the $1200, but the following year, the county received a check for $1200 signed by Ralph Street to compensate for the engineer's fee.

A correspondent for the Kansas City *Times* visited the doomed town of Linn Creek in March, 1931, and wrote this:

> This little town is in ruins. In a week or two, all that remains of it will be at the bottom of a lake fifty feet deep. The courthouse, the bank, the motion picture show, the First Baptist Church and the old homes where babies were born and elders died are little squares and rectangles of broken brick and stone. They are just like the ruins dug up from lava beds and deserts. Only the steps remain. One may sit upon them and brood on the desolate valley before the water comes.
>
> The water is creeping up now. It is coming very slowly, in little trickles. The fingers reach out into the dust, upward, upward. The old settler stoops and looks at it. He dabbles his fingers in a little pencil of water. He says, "That's nothing. That is just a drop of water. One could get that much from a bucket."

LINN CREEK BEFORE THE LAKE WATERS HAVE OVERFLOWED THE ENTIRE TOWN

Ah, but it was there to stay.. . . .

A few months ago Linn Creek was a flourishing town of more than 400 persons. It had stood there in the valley more than 75 years. The men and women who had been born there—and died there—loved it. It was the only reality upon the planet. It was the place they went away from and came back to. It was their home. They were embattled there, against the confusion of the great world...

Some sold. Others refused. The courts condemned. There is the right of eminent domain, you know. We said $10,000. Well, no. It's condemned now, you know. The evaluation committee says it's worth only $5000 . . .

The big company bought it. Boom! They blasted down the church and hauled away the timbers, leaving the great broken stones behind.

T. Victor Jeffries in his excellent book, "Before The Dam Waters," described the early history of the town and it's ultimate destruction. His personal collection of photographs is displayed in the Camden County Museum in Linn Creek, Missouri. Jeffries, who grew up in Old Linn Creek, worked for the power company in acquiring property in Linn Creek and told the author of the hostility he met when returning there. Many of the homes not moved from the town were burned. The last house to be burned there was the Henderson home with the telephone office upstairs. The photograph of the burning home is on the front cover of the novel, "Ashes," by the author. Stories of some of the experiences Jeffries had were relayed to the author in a conversation with him in the 1990's and are retold in the novel.

Here's J.W. Vincent writing about the demise of his town in the *Reveille*:

"The downtown portion of the old village is swiftly becoming a thing of the past . . . natives long ago, numbed or hardened to the fate of the old home town, watch an old familiar house consumed by flames with casual interest . . .

May as well laugh as cry."

The two smaller 3000-kilowatt water driven generators were in operation on April 23 and on May 4 the steam driven generators were shut down and the whole project was now running on hydropower.

As the dam neared completion, the town of Bagnell shrunk. The ferry that Ralph Street used eight years before to cross the Osage River in Bagnell was about to become history.

At four am, Saturday, May 30, 1931, the holiday then known as Decoration Day, ten-year-old Tennyson DeGraffenreid had the opportunity to make history, but he chose to stay in bed and sleep. His three aunts, Mrs. L.G. Degraffenreid of Kansas City, Kansas, and Misses Oma and Noma Degraffenreid of near Bagnell, climbed into a 1928 Chevrolet coach and drove toward the west end of the dam crossing designated as Highway 54. A steady rain hindered their progress and it took an hour to cover the five miles over dirt roads to reach the barriers across the newly completed concrete highway atop the half-mile-long power dam. According to the 50th Anniversary of Bagnell Dam book published by Union Electric in 1981, this account was given of the DeGraffenreid women's accomplishment:

> They sat there in the car while the rain was pouring down and waited patiently as they wished to be the first to cross the dam. So when the 6 am whistle blew they went speeding away over the big dam. While crossing they met four other cars and the Chevrolet sped away as the occupants strove to be the first to drive off the dam. When they arrived at the east end, they looked back across the lake and the others had not yet driven off the dam, so the three ladies went on their way very much elated to know that they were the first to cross the huge dam after the official opening to traffic.

The June 4, 1931 Eldon *Advertiser* reported a different story about the opening of Highway 54 across the dam. According to their article, Mrs. J.T. Ritter, superintendent at the Stone & Webster hospital at the dam, drove a new Auburn Eight across the dam from the east end and was the first to cross. The newspaper reported that Mrs. Ritter was given the spot in front of the other three cars waiting there because she had, "a good many friends," at the dam.

A total of 1774 automobiles followed the first five across the dam on that Saturday. On Sunday, 2914 automobiles crossed just to take a look at the marvel. Miller County Sheriff Abbott and the State Highway Department kept the traffic moving both days. A few boats were on the lake below the dam, one an old stern wheeled ferryboat taking passengers for tours.

By Saturday night the crowd of visitors to the dam overwhelmed the accomodations in Eldon. According to the Eldon *Advertiser*, by 8 pm all the hotel rooms in town were taken and 126 more people had called for rooms at the James House. Harold Yountz, the manager, called every home thought possible to accept tourists. Mayor J.H. Rea and other citizens took tourists into their homes for the night and provided breakfast the next morning. John Brockmeyer placed forty-two tourists in homes for the night. People were also placed in homes in Etterville, Barnett, and Versailles.

Farmers reported an influx of wild creatures fleeing the rising lake waters. Hunters claimed an invasion of foxes in the vicinity of Tuscumbia. Larger number of wolves were reported along the rivers leading into the lake. Union Electric employees tell of a large log they pulled from the water that split open exposing an enormous rattlesnake. The snake was said to have put up a vicious battle, but lost.

On June 7, George Haskell, plumbing foreman for Stone & Webster, was the first person reported drowned in the Lake of the Ozarks. On that Sunday morning, Mr. Haskell and a party of friends were fishing on the lake near Warsaw. When Mr. Haskell, who was reported to be an excellent swimmer, attempted to swim across the lake. He went under the water and was not seen again. He wore a pair of rubber boots thought to have been a factor in his drowning.

On June 1, the first two main generators had been phased in on Rivermines Number One transmission line. On July 1, main units three and four were phased in on Rivermines Number Two transmission line with the last two units phased in on July 17. Following the phase in of the units on the St. Louis Page Avenue lines, full generator tests started on August 6.

The Bagnell, Mo., ferry, which soon will become a thing of the past.

In Last Two Years Operators Have Made Profit Estimated Between $45,000 and $50,000.

The Jefferson City *Tribune* reported on the continuous and heavy feuding between farmers and the power company over the erosion of land along the Osage River below the dam. Later reports from the Army Corps of Engineers would indicate that an annual average of 29 acres of tillable land was being lost with the dam as a contributing factor.

Dr. James O. Walls, Miller County Health officer, and Frank Field, sanitary inspector, told of the mosquito control plan by Union Electric. The company used ten boats including six 24-foot workboats, three supervising speedboats and one large cabin cruiser that sprayed kerosene and crude oil on the lake to control the mosquito larvae. The boats were equipped with high-pressure sprayers. Places where the boats could not reach, men with knapsack sprayers completed the job on shore. The program was scheduled to begin each year in May and finish in October.

On a trip to the old town of Linn Creek, visitors found the town submerged with the lake front lapping at the door of Dr. Moore's house which was quite a ways up the creek and was being prepared to move to the new town called at the time, Estherville after the Esther family who owned the land. The sidewalks of the old town were being used as wharfs for speedboats and other watercraft. People looked down into the lake waters for sites they remembered. The lake was now 20 feet below full.

THE 150 TON CRANE PLACING THE ROTOR FOR GENERATOR INTO PLACE IN THE POWER STATION IN MAY, 1931.

The first commercial operation of the power plant started on October 16, 1931. "The Bagnell Dam is finished, Osage is on the line," announced the Union Electric Light and Power Company in full page advertisements in the St. Louis newspapers October 20.

"A vision has become a reality . . . the Osage River is harnessed in the service of mankind . . . tonight as you switch on your lights the power of the Osage leaps to do your bidding . . . OSAGE IS ON THE LINE!"

The Miller County *Autogram* reported that, "Tuscumbia people can remember when the Osage river was considered a menace to farmers who often worked hard at planting and tending corn only to see it wiped out by a flood."

Thomas Alva Edison died, October 18, 1931. His dream of providing direct current electricity to everyone had long ago been replaced by Nickola Tesla's promotion of alternating current.

County tax assessors from the four counties in which the lake was located were called to Jefferson City to meet with the State Tax Commission to work out the matter of assessing Bagnell Dam and the machinery located there and for the transmission lines. When the legislature had tried to pass legislation distributing the taxes based on a pro rata basis, Miller County officials objected because the dam itself is located in Miller County, but the county would receive practically no taxes on that plan.

Governor Caulfield met with the "hunger riders," a band of approximately 250 who marched on the capitol and demanded a special session of the Legislature to enact unemployment insurance and other relief measures, according to the St. Louis *Post-Dispatch*. The governor said that the state was doing everything it could to care for the unemployed. He called the problem, "essentially a local one and the local communities . . . are entirely able to care for those who are in need." He said the right of petition guaranteed by the Constitution did not include the right to march on the Capitol in force, "terrorizing towns and

TOWER FOR TRANSMISSION LINE TO RIVERMINES IN SOUTH-EAST MISSOURI

cities on the way and winding up with mobs riding through the streets of our capitol city." W.C. McCuistion of Kansas City, who admitted to being a member of the Communist party, headed the march.

Union Electric announced plans to begin a second transmission line from Bagnell Dam to St. Louis.

Development of hotels, resorts and schools on a grand scale on the 1300 mile shore line of the Lake of the Ozarks, was promised by Louis Egan, president of Union Electric in a speech before the Springfield Chamber of Commerce in December. Egan gave the listeners a vision of the "grandest recreation center in the Middle West," with modern hotels and reached by airlines from Kansas City and St. Louis.

"We are in this program to stay," Egan said of the plan to promote the area to tourists. He stated that Union Electric owned one-sixth of Camden County around the lake.

Union Electric filed a statement with the Miller County clerk and county assessor giving the figures for taxation purposes on Bagnell Dam real estate, equipment and transmission lines of $4,568,480 ($55,735,456). The figure increased the countywide assessed valuation by 40 percent. The county levy was 49 cents on $100, making Union Electric's taxes for the year of 1931, $22,386 ($273,104). The Miller County Court was of the opinion that the county levy could be reduced to 35 cents for the next year.

The condemnation suits in Camden County were drawing to a close in federal court under Judge Albert Reeves. Court appointed judges or appraisers awarded Camden County $31,015.80 ($378,392.76) for the courthouse and jail, almost $30,000 less than Missouri Hydro Electric offered to the county in 1926 in a contract Judge Skinker of the Circuit Court said was illegally signed by Presiding Judge Leonard Franklin. The appraisers awarded $19,710 ($240,462) for the six and one-half miles of roads in the Passover Road district and $1786 ($21,789) for two and one-half miles of roads in the Shawnee Bend road district. An award of $60,359 ($736,380) was made for outside road districts. Of the awards for roads that would be inundated by the lake, $26,520 was for state roads which Union

Electric challenged as not being under county supervision. Judge Reeves ultimately gave this amount back to Union Electric when he agreed that the county should not be awarded funds for state roads.

The state may transfer roads from county control to state control and the state had done so with the Camden County roads. The state highway commission had made a contract with Union Electric. Under this contract the highways had been adjusted, damages paid and bridges such as the span across the Glaize and across the dam had been constructed by the company.

Was the county entitled to damages because the road system was disturbed and the road distances made longer between certain points? The court ruled that the only right of the individual was to have reasonable access to the road system at some point and that any damages to the county as a governmental agency was so intangible and speculative that was impossible to ascertain.

On December 29, 1930, Camden County had taken exception to the appraisers' values and filed a motion asking for a trial by jury. The following March, however, the county withdrew their exceptions to the awards and reached an agreement with Union Electric after the company asked the court for a final judgment. When the judgment came down it carried these stipulations: For the company, they agreed to pay all accrued costs and would not make any further claims on them. Camden County agreed to accept as final and conclusive and fully binding upon the county the judgment of condemnation and agreed the company was entitled to all rights purported and expressed to have been obtained thereby and waived and discharged its rights on pending appeals.

Union Electric challenged the appraised values the judges gave the town of Linn Creek, claiming they were grossly excessive and greatly exceeded just compensation. The town received $12,907.10 ($154,892) for bridges and culverts, $4570 ($55,754) for sidewalks, and $5833.70 ($711,714), but was denied $19,264 ($235,020) for city streets as being not lawful items of damage according to Judge Reeves.

Damages were awarded for sewers, bridges and culverts because they were assessed on the theory that the city had actually expended money for them. Damages were later denied the town for sidewalks, curbs and streets as the expenditures for these were awarded to the owners of the abutting property.

Judge Reeves had driven the final nail in the coffin of the town of Linn Creek and those in Camden County opposing the dam.

OPTIONS, TRADES AND CONDEMNATION

THE SPEED and efficiency of the engineering and construction crews of Stone & Webster along with the Union Electric Light and Power Company worked against the lawyers and land buyers in Union Electric's land acquisition portion of the Osage Project. The engineers had set an initial completion date for the project for October 1931.

Cooperating weather conditions required few setbacks in the construction phase and the accuracy and efficiency of the engineering and planning for the project resulted in advancing the date for closing the gates in the dam first to June, then month by month, May, April, March until February 19, 1931 when the gates were finally closed and the lake began to fill.

The shrinking completion dates were like the tightening of a noose around the neck of the people in land acquisition. The Federal permit Walter Cravens had obtained to begin the dam and that continued under Union Electric and Stone and Webster, Permit Number 459MO, required approval by federal government engineers before the dam could be closed. The engineers required the basin of the lake to be cleared of timber and structures before that could occur. In addition, the State Health Department had issued the order for the Company to remove all the bodies buried in gravesites in the basin. But the land could not be cleared until the dam builders obtained title to the land. This requirement pitted the land acquisition crews against the engineers and construction crews. Could the lawyers shuffle the papers fast enough to keep up with the workmen pouring the concrete.

When Cravens and Guy Huston were forced out of the project and Missouri Hydro-Electric Company sold out to Union Electric, Burns and McDonnell Engineering Company had made a map of the affected area and an aerial survey had been made to check the accuracy of the map. The Company testified in the December 23, 1925 Public Service Commission hearing that they had acquired 30,000 acres of land, had 14,000 acres under contract and had options on 42,000 acres. The lake formed by the dam at that time was projected to impound 95 square mies or 60,800 acres. Before the project would be completed, Union Electric would acquire over 170,000 acres of land in six counties.

Twenty-five thousand acres of the land owned by Missouri Hydro-Electric was actually in the Farmers Fund, the corporation formed by Walter Cravens. This land went to the Kansas City Joint-Stock Land Bank and ultimately, after receivership, to the successor, the Phoenix Joint-Stock Land Bank.

Land acquired by fee simple was 109,000 acres. Only 7907 acres were acquired by condemnation. Condemnation was instituted whenever rightful ownership was not apparent or whenever a purchase price could not be negotiated with the owner.

R.R. Cox was in charge of land acquisition. Ralph Street found himself in the office set up by Union Electric in Kansas City to handle land acquisition and condemnation suits. The setup for handling acquisitions was divided into phases.

Phase one consisted of entering the name and number of the presumptive owner of a tract on a chart. Ownership was checked and opinion entered on status of the ownership, i.e. living, non-living, resident or non-resident, deceased heirs, minor heirs and other necessary information concerning the tract. Three offices and 25 investigators were employed to accomplish this in Linn Creek, Versailles and Warsaw.

The work advanced the property to Phase 2. When a survey of the property showing what part would be inundated and the exact courses and description furnished, the property was entered in Phase 3.

When the supervisor had all the information gathered and on his desk, a registered letter was sent along with a formal offer to buy the necessary easement with an amount of the offer and a time for the offer to be accepted.

This put the tract in Phase 4. Phase 5 came when the time had expired for acceptance. During this time, the land department was negotiating with the owner. If the time to accept the offer had expired, the supervisor made the decision whether or not to enter the tract into litigation by condemnation. If this was done, the tract was in Phase 6 and an attorney was assigned to draw a petition and a suit was filed. If the land department reported that the tract had been sold before it went to litigation, the file was sent to the office devoted to closing contracts and the chart was changed to show the land had been purchased.

Three hundred and forty-two tracts were listed for condemnation. Ultimately, 235 parcels were condemned. Not all condemnation suits were over price disputes. In some cases there were title defects where no living person could convey a good title.

The question of legality on the subject of eminent domain arose from the very beginning of the condemnation process.

That question was put to rest and condemnation suits were allowed to continue following the decision by the United States Federal Court, Central Division of Western District of Missouri that the Osage Project constituted a "superior public use," as defined in the Federal Water Powers Act of 1920 that was enacted by Congress and by the license granted to the builders of the dam by the Federal Power Commission. Under that act, jurisdiction for Condemnation was given to Federal Courts when the amount claimed exceeded $3000. The rule used by the land acquisition people was that in cases where the owner of the property asked $2000 or more, those claims were brought in the Federal District Court and claims of lesser amounts went to the county where the property existed.

When Donald Fitch talked in the December 23, 1925 hearing by the Public Service Commission about acquiring the property in Linn Creek, he said, "We have paid most liberally for all the property that we have acquired in Linn Creek . . . We have paid more for that property than it was worth . . ."

Sam Haley asked, "Well, in what way have you acquired that property?"

Fitch responded, "Well, we have acquired a lot of it by outright purchase and some of it by option."

Haley, "By trade?"

Fitch, "We have traded some for it."

A land buyer for the hydro company told of an incident he witnessed: "A woman was signing her deed and receiving her check which was for a sum far in excess of anything she would have suspected two years previous. Yet such is human nature that she was bemoaning the little she was to get for the old place. Another woman listened for awhile before interrupting to remark, 'Well, I certainly don't feel thataway. We've got a new farm contracted for that's just as good as the old and at half the price we're going to get and nearer to town and schools, too. I just hope to God nothing keeps me from getting over tothat table to sign the deed."

In Carl Herbert Schwartz's *Financial Study of the Joint-Stock Land Banks*, he claims that certain joint-stock land banks established "farmers' funds" for the purpose of taking over the undesirable assets and had involved questionable practices that had resulted in indictments of their officers on criminal charges.

Donald Fitch was asked by Judge Ing of the Public Service Commission, "What is the Farmers Fund, Incorporated?"

Fitch identified it as, "a trading medium that operated without profit. It was a separate corporation which took certain lands from the Kansas City Joint-Stock Land Bank, which they had taken under foreclosure, and traded these lands for other lands in the project, paying cash into the Land Bank."

Fitch identified 8707 acres of farm land in Missouri and Kansas as being land that had been foreclosed on by the bank. In a March 1928 letter to the Commission, Robert Webb of the Webb Motor Company of Linn Creek told of his experiences in "land trading," with the Missouri Hydro-Electric Company. "I was told by agents of the company's holding corporation that unless I optioned or traded my farm near Zebra, condemnation proceedings would be instituted within thirty days, that the matter would be handled in Kansas City and that I would have to take what I could get, regardless of whether the appraisers knew anything about what the property was worth or not. (I) was induced to believe that the dam might be built and sold my farm at a reduced price, taking part in trade as many others did."

F. H. Krahle, the Linn Creek barber, told the St. Louis *Globe-Democrat* how the company came around wanting to trade. "They are willing to trade anything from a whetstone to a farm in Australia, but I never see any cash changing hands. Trade, trade, that's all we hear. For what? For a farm and I'm no farmer and never want to be."

THE BANKS

FINANCING THE DAM turned out to be the most controversial element in completing Bagnell Dam. Walter Cravens and Alice B. Todd got caught trying to get the financing done without following the rules. In a way, they helped write the rules that followed the debacle they created at the Kansas City Joint Stock Land Bank. This chapter is a review of sorts of what transpired at that bank and what repercussions followed.

The Joint Stock Land Banks were private mortgage bond companies operated for profit and chartered under the authority of the Federal Farm Loan Act of 1916. Here, Walter Cravens put his talk about millions of dollars to practice. He put the small agricultural loans behind him and started dealing in the big bucks.

The joint stock land banks were capitalized at $250,000 ($3.037,500) or more and received no help from the government by way of capital subscription. Cravens borrowed the money to get the bank started in Salina through the mortgage company his father had started, then took over the loans the mortgage company had on its books. The original law on the joint stock land banks did not limit the size of the loans, but an amendment to the Act in 1923 limited them to loans to agricultural purposes only and reduced the size of the loans to $50,000 ($607,500). The federal government appraised the farm and the loan was limited to a percentage of the value of the land and buildings.

During the Congressional Hearing on House Resolution 9433 in 1930, Congressman Fitzpatrick criticized the appraisal part of the farm loan act and blamed it for the failures that were occurring in the joint stock land banks, including Cravens' Kansas City bank.

"The (Farm Loan) board put in the receivership and declared the bank insolvent. Afterwards (they) reappraised these farms, the basis of the bank's assets, on a basis which, I say to you, if it was a fair basis should have been the basis of the original appraisement. It is not a fair basis to be now substituted to ruin the stockholders."

Mr. Albert C. Williams of the Federal Farm Loan Board responded at the Congressional Hearing March, 1930, on the receivership of Joint Stock Land Banks under the Federal Farm Loan Act: "I want you to know that a determined effort was made, in cooperation with the Treasury and the Department of Justice, to ascertain the condition of the Kansas City Joint Stock Land Bank and to bring about proper adjustments in connection with reported irregularities. These efforts were strongly opposed by certain officers and directors of the bank. While the audit was in progress almost continuously for more than 12 months prior to the date of appointment of a receiver, the auditors reported that it was necessary to submit financial and operating statements without certifications to their accuracy . . . I think it will be sufficient to say that anyone familiar with the record will concur in the view that the action of the board in appointing a receiver was fully justified."

The for-profit joint stock land banks profited until farmland prices declined in the early twenties. Cravens was asked about the decline during his trial. He told the court that in the latter part of 1923, the Kansas City Joint Stock Land Bank controlled 100 to 125 farms that had been foreclosed on. That was when Cravens said he started a new company, the Missouri-Kansas Farms Company to manage the foreclosed farms. The deflation of farm values continued through 1924-25 and land banks throughout the country came into ownership of considerable amount of real estate.

On April 25, 1925, Cravens started the infamous Farmers Fund Company that Ralph Street had tried to explain to the Public Service Commission and that J.W. Vincent later wrote about in the *Reveille*:

"The 'dam company's land' to which reference is often made, was once held by the Farmers Fund Incorporated and upon collapse of the Kansas City Joint Stock Land Bank, to which these lands rightfully belonged, restitution was demanded and the lands conveyed to the bank and still in the receiver's hand."

The creation of a farmers fund company was probably not an original idea of Cravens'. The First Report of Receiver reprinted in the Eleventh Annual Report of the Federal Farm Loan Board of 1927 said this about such companies:

"The use of so-called 'Farmers' Funds' or farm companies for the purpose of taking over the undesirable assets of certain joint stock land banks had been used by other banks and had involved some questionable practices which had resulted in indictments of their officers on criminal charges."

The Report said about the Kansas City Joint Stock Land Bank:

"The report of the receiver indicates that the condition of the bank was such as to make its closing inevitable. The difficulties which the bank encountered and the losses which had been sustained were in large measure the fault of the management. Statements had been falsified, funds misappropriated, and quality of business sacrificed for the sake of volume. In order to conceal the true condition of the bank, affiliated companies were organized to take over real estate so that such assets continued to appear as mortgage loans on the bank's books."

Rumors of difficulty in joint stock land banks were around during 1925 and 1926 and led to the invasion of examiners in December 1925 at the Kansas City bank. Dividends were discontinued in a number of the banks and stock prices plummeted. The Treasury Department began an investigation in the matter and, helped out by what they found in Cravens accounting books, one conclusion of land bank problems was a lack of uniformity in accounting and financial practices among the banks. Different methods were used in arriving at earnings, which in turn influenced dividend policies. An interesting phase of the problem was that certain banks—again, including the Kansas City bank—used new stock premiums to bulk up dividends of old stock purchases. A practice that could not be sustained for any length of time.

1927 marked the end of a ten-year period of the farm loan system and nine years of Cravens farm loan bank. Three joint stock land banks were placed in receivership that year including the Kansas City bank on May 4. The Farm Loan Bureau was completely reorganized that year—thanks in part by the activities the examiners had uncovered in Cravens' 12th floor elaborate banking office. Three of the seven members of the Farm Loan Board were asked to resign by the President and were replaced immediately. The inadequacy of bank examinations in the case of the joint stock land banks became evident in the case of the Kansas City bank.

The 12 month long investigation of Cravens' bank under the leadership of Nugent Dodds led to eventual receivership. Attempts were made to bring about adjustments there, but Cravens' management strongly opposed them. When the bank defaulted on bond interest payments on May 1, and failed to comply with the Farm Loan Board's request that additional collateral be deposited as security for the bank's bonds, a receiver was appointed.

January 14, 1929, saw a gathering of Herman Langworthy, receiver of the Kansas City Joint Stock Land Bank, Massey Holmes, attorney for the bondholders protective committee, Walter McLucas, chairman of the bondholders committee and a representative of the stockholders for a meeting with the Federal Farm Loan Board. The bondholders brought with them a plan for reorganizing the bank. Langworthy said if the plan was ultimately approved, the bank would continue to operate.

The next month was when Langworthy went to federal court in Kansas City to petition the court to sort out the financial maze Walter Cravens and Miss Alice B. Todd had left the bank in. Henry L. Jost, receiver for the Missouri-Kansas Farms Company had already sued the bank for $600,000 ($7,290,000) that the company claimed the bank owed them. The Cravens Mortgage, also in receivership, asked the court for a lesser amount. Langworthy's petition made the same claims about the bank's transactions the government made in the trial and conviction of Cravens and Miss Todd the previous year, that "Illegal and improper transactions" were made in order to reflect a false statement of earnings of the bank. The transactions were, Langworthy declared, "interlocked, enmeshed and complicated."

What came out of the Federal Farm Loan Board meeting slammed a crushing blow to the 1800 stockholders of the bank on March 23. The board, which had listened to plans submitted by the bondholders, the stockholders and Langworthy in January, followed Langworthy's recommendation and assessed a 100 percent levy on the stockholders. Langworthy said the bank's deficit was $6,498,812.62 ($78,960573.33). The stockholders would have to come up with $100 per share, the par value of the stock. Some stockholders had paid as much as $180 per share for the stock.

The inflated price was a result of the creative bookkeeping employed by Cravens and Miss Todd and high-pressure tactics used by sales organization and was what led to the indictment of Cravens, Guy Huston and six others by a federal grand jury in Massachusetts the previous year. Several congressional inquiries and hearings, plus the reorganizations of the Farm Loan Board were the outcomes of the "double indemnity" of the stockholders because they were voicing their displeasure en masse to their congressmen.

The bulk of the issues of Cravens' bank stock was held in eastern states, New York, Massachusetts and Pennsylvania, as well as Ohio, Michigan, Illinois and California. Few of the stockholders were located close to Cravens hometown of Salina, Kansas.

Langworthy expressed confidence in the ability to reorganize the bank and put it on a profitable basis.

One month following the public announcement of the "double

whammy" against the stockholders was when Massachusetts Representative George R. Stobbs made his call for a congressional investigation of the Kansas City Joint Stock Land Bank.

Investors said they had made the assumption the banks were government institutions because the certificates contained the statement that they were " instrumentality's of the Government of the United States," and were "under federal supervision." The terms were meant to apply to the tax exemption feature of their bonds and mortgages. No doubt this phrase was used by more aggressive salesmen despite the effort of the Farm Loan Board and the American Association of Joint Stock Land Banks to educate the public as to the correct meaning..

"Unfortunately, the securities of joint stock land banks are not government bonds, nor in any wise legally guaranteed by the United States," Stobbs said. "Many of them were sold under representation they were virtually government bonds."

A.O. Stewart, a San Francisco financier, entered the drama of the Kansas City bank later in the year. He came forward with three alternatives to resurrect a Missouri-Kansas Joint Stock Land Bank.

Stewart's offer to structure a new bank required a 95 percent participation of bondholders in the Kansas City bank. The bonds could be turned in for 60 cents on the dollar or they could be traded for new bonds at a reduction of 15 percent off the face value of the old bonds. The old bonds could be turned in for 5 percent bonds or a 4 1/2 percent bond coupled with stock participation in the new Stewart company. The stockholders would pass out of the picture, losing their entire investment, but would be relieved of the "double liability" of being assessed the par value of their stock, thus gaining the favor of large investors.

Stewart was the president of the Pacific Coast Joint Stock Land Bank and controlled the Salt Lake City Joint Stock Land Bank. The plan would give Stewart 60 percent of the stock in the new Kansas City venture. Forty percent of the common stock would be available to the bondholders who elected to go with that portion of the plan. At the time of election there were $44,376,500 ($539,174,475) in outstanding bonds. The Farm Loan approved the plan, as did the bondholders and stockholders committees.

In addition to setting up a new joint stock land bank with headquarters in Kansas City, a liquidation company would be created.

Stewart's financial backer in the enterprise was the Bank of Italy. In January 1931, Stewart announced that 97 percent of the bondholders in the Kansas City Joint Stock Land Bank had elected to participate in his plan.

The rebirth of the land bank occurred in June 1931 when Stewart bid a pre-arranged $26,759,000 ($325,012,500) for the assets of the Kansas City Joint Stock Land Bank. The staged auction took place in Walter Cravens' luxurious digs on the 12th floor of Land Bank Building he built in 1924 to house his, then, $50 million enterprise. Cravens had sold $44 million in farm loans and $3.8 million in stock, all of which was lost by the stockholders. The auction transferred the $26,750,000 in assets from the old bank to the newly formed bank named the Phoenix Joint Stock Land Bank, with the remaining assets going into the liquidation company Stewart formed.

"This will be the cleanest joint stock land bank in the entire system," Stewart said. "It will have no real estate. Its assets will be in selected hand-picked loans in good standing."

The final liquidating dividends were disbursed to the bondholders in November, 1931. As a result of the severe depression in the country at that time, the bondholders realized only $61.33 per $100 bond. Langworthy, in 1928 had estimated a return of $93 per $100 bond while Stewart had promised $60 in his plan. Stewart formed the First, Second and Third Joint Stock Land Banks in Kansas City as well as the Phoenix Joint Stock Land Bank and took over the mortgages with the Missouri Farm Mortgage Company. Immediately thereafter, the Phoenix Bank took over the other three banks. A clause in the charter of the banks allowed loaning activities in up to five states in case of consolidation instead of the two states the original bank had been restricted to.

The Emergency Farm Mortgage Act of 1933 ordered the joint stock land banks to liquidate and provided funds to accomplish it with the Farm Credit Act.

Many of the condemnation suits were combined in case number 233, including the case against the town of Linn Creek and the one against Camden County. One of the early ones settled was against the First National Bank in which Union Electric paid the bank and the owners $13,918. In all of the suits, the court appointed three judges who inspected the property and gave an appraised value which the court accepted and usually the property owner did also. Not so, of course, the case against Linn Creek nor the one against the county.

The appraisers gave these values to the court for settlement against the town of Linn Creek, but Union Electric made exceptions to the court that the allowance to the town was "grossly excessive and greatly exceeded just compensation." The court sided with Union Electric that the streets in the town were not lawful items of damage. As the town burned, building by building with only a few of the houses off their foundations and on conveyances to move to the new town of Linn Creek or the new location of the county seat, with the lots shorn of trees and with the river ready to rise and cover all, the history book of Old Linn Creek was on its final page.

Finis!

The county's contentious relationship with the dam builders finally came to a close as the generators at the new powerhouse in the completed dam began turning out current for consumption in St. Louis and the Rivermines in Southeast Missouri.

TODD vs CRAVENS

EXACTLY WHEN Alice Barbara Todd and Walter Price Cravens met is unclear. Salina, Kansas was, and still is, a small town where everyone knows everyone else. Cravens' father was a businessman and seemed to be well respected in the community. Alice's first acknowledgement under oath about her relationship with Walter was that it occurred in 1917 when he enticed her—implied by her testimony—to join him in forming a joint stock land bank there in Salina.

One could presume Cravens' plans called for someone he could confide in and trust to carry out his intention to amass the fortune he had been talking about. That she was complicit in his maneuverings in juggling funds among his various enterprises was well documented in their trial, by her own admission. What she wasn't forthcoming about until later was just exactly how in detail they actually did conspire and how their intentions about the outcome of the Missouri Hydro Electric Company matched.

Apparently, by Miss Todd's testimony later under oath, the two had an arrangement of some kind of kickback scheme wherein she was giving money back to Cravens out of a salary he promised her beginning in 1919 after he had named her secretary of the land bank. She was to say it was $150 (although, once under oath she put the amount at $125) per month until 1924 when it was increased to $200 per month. This continued until 1930, according to Miss Todd, although she received no salary from the land bank after it went into receivership in 1927. Where the $200 came from and why she was still giving it to her no-longer boss is open to speculation.

Following the conviction of Walter Cravens and Alice B. Todd in June, 1928 in the Federal District Court of the Western Division, Miss Todd's two brothers-in-law, William Wakefield and Robert Muir loaned Cravens and Miss Todd $1500 in August, 1928 apparently to help with their legal battle. After their indictment in 1927, Wakefield and Muir had already made a loan of $2500 for their legal expenses with both Miss Todd and Cravens signing for the loan. The title to a piece of land in Linn Creek was held by Wakefield and Muir as security for the loan.

Cravens sent a letter to Wakefield dated August 11, 1928 as follows:

> *Dear Will,*
>
> *I have been so tied up with work the past week that I have been unable to write you regarding the loan which you and your brother in law made me over the Linn Creek property.*
>
> *The cost of the transcript of such a record for the appeal court can hardly be conceived by anyone not familiar with the case. The estimate is that there will be about five thousand sheets and the cost of Federal Court appeal work is sixty cents per sheet. We had an understanding that the reporters would keep us in the financing of this work but it seems that after the trial was over they took advantage of our situation and forced us to put up the money in advance, which was indeed embarrassing and of course your loan has made it possible for us to go ahead with the work. I assure you that I appreciate it from the bottom of my heart and will see that it is paid.*
>
> *We have every confidence in the outcome of the appeal. As we see it and as our friends and many able*

lawyers tell us, this is the only place where we can expect justice. It is doubtful if the decision will be made in a year, probably a year and a half. In the meantime we are going ahead with our work and trying to rebuild our lost fortunes and get back to normal living.

Thanking you again for your assistance and interest and with kind regard to yourself and your family I am

Very Truly yours,
Walter Cravens.

The year 1930 found Miss Todd in Minneapolis, MN. She claimed that Cravens had promised her a salary of $200 a month to sell real estate there for him, a salary that he apparently never paid her. The 1930 census counted her as a resident of that city. It was in January, 1930, as Miss Todd said in the suit she would later file, that Cravens had intervened in Case Number 1365 in Federal District Court between Missouri Hydro Electric Power Company vs H.M. Langworthy, Receiver of the Kansas City Joint Stock Land Bank declaring that $530,153.63 was due him for his interest in the Power Company. A claim that she said on March 6, 1931 Cravens settled for the sum of $300,000.

Alice B. Todd's exasperation with her former boss had to have been near the breaking point, what with all the money she had given, loaned and claimed to have recorded on the bank's books as salary, but that had really gone into Cravens' pocket, and with the oral agreement she said they had made in 1924 that she was to share in proceeds from the Missouri Hydro-Electric project; after all the false transactions she had made at his instructions in funneling money over to the dam project, he was now reneging on his promise to cut her in for 25 percent of the $300,000.

In April, 1931 a series of letters were exchanged between Cravens and William Wakefield. Miss Todd's frustration with her former boss is brought out in the letters between the two men who seemed—at least in the beginning exchange—to be quite collegiate with each other. as well they might be in a small town. The Wakefields lived just down the street in Salina from Cravens' mother in a house he might possibly have called home at one time. The letters are part of the case file and are useful to portray Cravens—especially—in a manner that would seem to fit well with the schemes he was associated with.

Barons House
C. H. MARTIN, PROP.
CONCORDIA, KANSAS Apr 15, 1931

Mr Walter Cravens
 Kansas City Mo —
Dear friend Walter —
 Realizing that you have had troubles aplenty I have had no desire to harass you in regard to your debt to me. I hope now that your problems are nearing solution and that the reorganization of the bank with settlement of your claims against it will enable you to make payment — This would be a Godsend to me as I have lost heavily on land investments and I do not have the money to pay the next interest installment which is due on May 14 next — which is the third anniversary of my debt for while I was glad to be able to help and did it willingly I borrowed the $2500⁰⁰ and I have

not been "able" to repay it. You will recall that I returned to you for your use the securities which you sent with your note.

Also from time to time I have furnished Alice money which she expected to repay from her participation in bank settlements; has she a prospect of being able to do this?

I will very much appreciate your telling me what I may expect.

TODD vs CRAVENS 203

MISSOURI CENTRAL CONSTRUCTION CO.
404 COMMERCE TRUST BUILDING
KANSAS CITY, MO.

sphone, HArrison 4831

May 8, 1931.

Mr. Wm. Lakefield,
745 South Santa Fe Ave.,
Salina, Kansas.

Dear Will:

I intended to reply to your letters earlier in the week, but owing to a death in the family of a friend, I just have not been able to get to it.

It is difficult for me to write you as frankly as I would like, as I do not know just where I stand just now, owing to the fact that Alice has informed me that she intends to bring some sort of a suit against me, also it rather goes without saying that your inquiry was either prompted or inspired by her, which is quite all right.

There is no possibility of a settlement with the bank, whereby they will pay any money. We have simply been maneuvered into a position where we cannot continue the prosecution of our suits, owing principally to lack of funds, etc. At this time also, the matter of expenses of the appeal is before me, the arrangements for which have not been finally completed

I have not ignored nor forgotten about the $2500.00 note to which you refer, but it has not been possible for me to do anything about it, on account of the existing conditions. It is not my intention to overlook it, and I do not want you to think for a minute that I do not appreciate what you have done, and if you really are concerned over the ultimate payment of this note, I shall be very glad to have a talk with you at the first opportunity, for reasons as stated above; I just do not know what to write under the present conditions, in the way of discussing my future plans. I have no fear but what I will be able to satisfy you; however, if the suit I referred to is filed, it might result in placing me in a position where I could not do things as I would like to. It seems to me it would be most unfortunate if you should become the victim of a misunderstanding. I assure you that I will do all I can to avoid anything of that kind.

I am extremely sorry that I am unable to be of assistance to you at this time, but, Will, I have had no means of income, and am just getting myself straightened around. We have yet a terrible fight before us, and upon the outcome depends everything in the world, and the matter of expenses and fees are very heavy, and I am letting no stone go unturned to win this battle. I am sure upon reflection that you will appreciate and understand the situation.

With kindest regards, I am

Yours very truly,

Walter Cravens

WC:B

May 12, 1931 -

Dear Walter - I appreciate your letter of the 8th. I will be candid with you and you may be equally frank with me. Alice and I are not in collusion nor is I backing her in anything that she may do. I have furnished her money at different times, some since she went to Minneapolis. She has always represented that there were claims of the Casualty Co and the Finance Co against the bank from which there would be funds in which she would share and could then repay me. In various letters she has made reference to the refinancing of the bank and the prospect of these settlements being made. She wrote some time ago that she had the information that these claims had been settled and money paid but that she had apparently been left out and intended demanding settlement. I think it most unfortunate if there is to be a breach after all that you have gone through together. It should not be. My letter to you was simply and purely from my own interest and on the supposition that the above mentioned information was correct. The last thing that I desire is misunderstanding or lack of cordial feeling. I have sympathized with your position and continually defended both you and Alice and I do not now regret having helped as I did regardless of the outcome. And if my financial condition was as I hoped and expected it to be would gladly write this off and forget it. As it is now am flooded with matters above present income, with prospect of having to sacrifice a fine at a heavy loss. But at that my difficulty is my financial whereas you have the other battle in addition in which I trust for your success. Will appreciate hearing further.

BLACK RIVER HYDRO-ELECTRIC CO.
KANSAS CITY, MISSOURI

601 COMMERCE BLDG.

HArrison 4831

August 12, 1931.

Mr. W. S. Wakefield,
745 South Santa Fe,
Salina, Kansas.

Dear Will:

I have your letter of August 8. I know of no way that I could make any kind of a security settlement that would release Miss Todd from the note. I presume what you mean is that if I would put up some kind of collateral, you would release her, but unfortunately I am not in position to do this. I do not know of any way that Miss Todd can sue me on an obligation due you; of course she can try.

The outcome of the Linn Creek property was that the sale to James Banner did not materialize, owing to the fact that the Land Bank claimed the property. Something over a year after this deal had fallen through, the property was sold to the power company at St. Louis for $3500.00, which included the payment of a $2000.00 mortgage. The receiver of the bank tied up the sale by litigation; the mortgagee started foreclosure proceedings on the mortgage; the wind-up was a compromise, and the mortgagee collected the amount of the mortgage, and the balance was paid to the Receiver of the Land Bank.

I am not sure that I understand your letter correctly, as you seem to be of a disposition to support Miss Todd in her suit. Of course that is your right. I want to refer you to my letter of May 8th, in which I outlined my position as plain as I could. You are a business man, Will, and I know you are fair. The trouble is you do not understand, or rather do not have any conception of some of the difficulties that are involved in this whole deal. The money you have advanced on that note is a very small part of the amount involved, and yet I have no controversy with the others; all are entirely in accord with the plan of liquidation.

I want to impress upon you that, in my judgment, if any suit is filed, you probably never will get your money, and I think I could convince you of that in five minutes if I could see you. For instance, I have never told the others that there was any pressure being brought, and I am sure that any hostile move would tend to place you in a position where I could not ask any favors. I have not told my lawyers, even, about your end of it, except I have advised them that Miss Todd had informed me she was going to sue me, and naturally I employed counsel for proper protection, and as stated in my letter of May 8, and outlined above, it would surely be unfortunate if you should be one of the victims of the existing misunderstanding, and a misunderstanding which I have no way of adjusting.

With kindest regards, I am

Yours truly,

WC:B

HARTELY & CO.
ENGINEERS
▼
KANSAS CITY, MISSOURI

601 COMMERCE BLDG.   HArrison 4831

August 13, 1931.

Mr. W. S. Wakefield,
745 South Santa Fe,
Salina, Kansas.

Dear Will:

I happened to glance over a copy of the letter I wrote you yesterday, and it occurs to me you might get the wrong interpretation of the statement I made in the first paragraph, concerning the matter of collateral. The impression I intended to leave with you was not that I would not put up any collateral, but that I could not, for the reason that I did not own any.

If my business matters continue to progress as they are, it is possible that I may be able to make some arrangement later on that would be satisfactory in the event I am not able to liquidate the note sooner.

I just thought I would write you again, as I would not have you feel that I was at all arbitrary on the point.

Yours truly,

Salina Ks 8/15/31

Mr Walter Cravens — KC

Dear Walter — I am glad to have received your second letter before answering yours of the 12th which somehow did not seem over cordial and the reference to remote of possible suit could easily be interpreted as a threat. Regardless of what my sympathy or opinion might be I am not supporting Alice in her suit by either counsel or finance. My position and attitude are as expressed in my letter of May 12th.

You speak of other creditors as being satisfied or in accord with the plan of liquidation but you know Walter this is the first mention of it to me. I have no knowledge of the extent of the obligations or to whom owing or what the plan of liquidation may be that you mention. I should like to know the latter as I am faced with the necessity of making some kind of program of readjustment financially with a view to reduce the interest burden which is too great for my present income.

Cordially yours
J. T. W.

BLACK RIVER HYDRO-ELECTRIC CO.
KANSAS CITY, MISSOURI

601 COMMERCE BLDG.　　　　　　　　　　　　　　　HArrison 4831

August 21st, 1931.

Mr. W. S. Wakefield,
745 So. Santa Fe Ave.,
Salina, Kans.

Dear Will:

　　　　　I was glad to receive your letter of the 15th and to know that you have not misconstrued any of my letters. My only point in saying what I did about the suit is simply this; I had in mind the future and that in event that things go against us, and all of our troubles have to be balanced in red ink, and it should be found that things could have been managed differently by some constructive co-operation, etc., if such things should happen that way, then I would have the satisfaction of knowing that I had at least warned you.

　　　　　I am surprised to know that you are not aware of the fact that there are other creditors, as I assumed Alice had given you some idea as to some of our problems. I don't believe that I could give you a fair idea as to what I am trying to do by way of a letter. Then again I do not dare to just now Will; in view of the fact that I am faced with litigation. I have not asked my attorneys, but I know that they would not permit me to do it. There is no reason, however, why you should not have the information. There are many, many problems and complications which have to be worked out and it is with much difficulty that I write or do anything when I am faced with a suit, but I am sure you can appreciate that.

　　　　　I don't want you to lose your money. I want to do all I can to help, but I cannot do the impossible. I suggest this. I have to be away for some little time to come, possibly more or less for a month, but at some time during the month of September I am expecting to have some important information that will have considerable bearing on my affairs. This may be delayed more than a month, however.

　　　　　Sometime during the month of September I will try and arrange to come out to Salina and go over the entire matter with you or failing in that possibly you might arrange to drop down here on a Saturday or I might arrange to meet you somewhere on your route. It runs in my mind that you travel east of Salina. This I will take up with you later.　　Yours very truly,

Dear Walter

Had expected to be in KC last month and see you as suggested in your letter of May 2 but did not get down. Of course I had some knowledge of the developments in your affairs and while you still have your problems and very serious ones too, so do I have some. Your ability to do things in a big way and the size of your transactions make my financial affairs look trivial perhaps but they are none the less vital to me. As I have told you before things have broken badly for me and I have not been able to reduce my load. I have my mother's loan to keep up beside my own, my farmers are unable to pay their rent and crops will not pay my taxes — so have borrowed to pay taxes and to pay interest. As to your loan I borrowed that money (when you were in need) and have not been able to repay it. Have paid four full years interest and due mother six months installment 11/1/1c. and it is not just that I should be compelled to continue carrying it. My circumstances make it imperative that I ask you for settlement now in which Robt. shares. Hoping to hear from you favorably
I am as ever
Yours very truly
WEM

HARTLEY & CO.
ENGINEERS

KANSAS CITY, MISSOURI

601 COMMERCE BLDG.   HARRISON 4831

October 26, 1931.

Mr. W. S. Wakefield,
Salina, Kansas.

Dear Will:

I have your letter of the 24th. Am sorry that you have been unable to get to Kansas City. I do not believe that the proper picture of the situation can be obtained by correspondence.

There is no way that it would be possible for me to make any settlement on the note at the present time. In fact, I am confronted with the matter of further expenditures in our litigation and the filing of additional motions, etc., and these are problems that I have not worked out as yet.

I had thought that I would be able to get out there, but it has not been possible. If you should find a way to get down here, drop me a line a week or so in advance as I am out of town frequently, and without much notice. The responsibility of working out our problems here is entirely upon my shoulders, and I have to do it as best I can, and I feel that I have accomplished a good deal this year - even though it might not appear so to others. Anyhow, I should be very glad indeed to have the opportunity of talking matters over with you.

With kindest regards to yourself and Mrs. Wakefield, I am

Yours very truly,

Walter Cronin

WC:L

On November 2, 1931, Cravens incorporated as Hartley and Company, thereby putting the $300,000 out of reach for all claims against him personally. That, possibly, was the final slap that Alice B. Todd was going to endure. The tight pact and relationship between them, so touted in the press coverage during the federal case against the two, began to publicly fall apart on March 11, 1932, when William S. Wakefield and Robert A. Muir filed an involuntary bankruptcy case against Cravens in federal court. The two alleged that Cravens owed them $4000 on two promissory notes. The petitioners wanted payment for the note dated August 8, 1928 and due February 4, 1929 for $1500 and one for $2500 dated May 14, 1927 and due on demand, plus eight percent interest.

Cravens responded with a motion for dismissal of the involuntary bankruptcy petition before Judge Merrill E. Otis on March 24. His attorney asked for the dismissal on grounds that the petition was insufficient. The petition, in the claim for dismissal, lacked any proof that Cravens was insolvent at the time he was alleged to have been concealing his assets from his creditors. Six days later Judge Otis ruled in favor of Cravens and allowed twenty days for the filing of an amended petition.

Wakefield and Muir filed an amended petition on April 2, alleging that Cravens borrowed $100,000 from a Kansas City bank in March 1931, and bought real estate at 1116 Baltimore Avenue for $120,000. A second transaction involved property at 1228 Main Street that included the Loews' Midland Theater for $30,000. Cravens, the petition claimed, concealed his assets by accomplishing the transactions in the name of a concern known as Hartley and Company.

Not all of the news was dark for Miss Todd and Cravens. Nugent Dodds and the Justice Department had decided on January 19, 1932 to drop the indictments the two grand juries had returned in 1927 against them and Ralph Street, along with the other seven individuals and the various Cravens' companies. Case 7957 terminated any further court action in connection with the charges from the indictments. Cra vens and Miss Todd, however, still had the prison sentences hanging over them. Street had escaped the legal problems that Cravens had brought on the entire organization.

The spat continued though, when Cravens fired back at Wakefield and Muir on April 6 with a suit for $100,000 damages on the charge of conspiracy to injure Hartley and Company. The suit was filed against Wakefield and Muir, but added the name of a Minneapolis real estate man named Louis Wille. Representing Hartley and Company was, who else, Henry Conrad, Cravens' favorite attorney, assisted by Hale Houts and C.H. Kohler. The statements against Cravens and his alleged connection with the company were false, the suit claimed, and the petition by the two Salina men and the Minneapolis real estate man was causing great harm to Hartley and Company.

Kohler admitted that Cravens was a "small" stockholder in Hartley and Company (note the letterhead used by Cravens for the letters he wrote to Wakefield the previous year), but that he had nothing to do with the purchase of the two real estate properties. The suit said that the petitioners for the involuntary bankruptcy suit against Cravens the previous month had entered into a conspiracy to injure Hartley and Company. Named as part of the conspiracy was H.C. Doyle, attorney for Wakefield and Muir, but Doyle was not named as a defendant in the suit.

On April 14, 1932, the court battle led to an open split between Cravens and Miss Todd when she jumped into the fray by filing suit in the Independence, Missouri division of the circuit court for her share of the $300,000 ($3,645,000) she said was paid Cravens by the Union Electric Light and Power Company when they purchased the assets of the Missouri Hydro-Electric Power Company in 1929.

"I should have brought suit for it long ago," she told the Kansas City *Times* at 745 South Santa Fe Avenue in Salina, the home of her sister, Gertrude, Mrs. William S. Wakefield. "My claim is made against settlements Mr. Cravens received some months ago in connection with the hydro-electric project. Those settlements totaled between $300,000 and one-half million dollars. I am aware that many people, especially in Salina, believe Mr. Cravens now has no funds, but I know differently."

Counsel for Cravens filed a formal request for a transfer of the case to the Kansas City Circuit Court, which Judge Jasper Bell overruled. He then granted a change of venue upon an additional request and sent the case to Division Three for a hearing.

Doyle and Conrad clashed again in the Kansas City, Kansas, Federal Court in June when Judge John C. Pollock appointed B.J. Sheridan as receiver for the Cravens Mortgage Company in Salina, Kansas, where Walter Cravens began his financial career. Petitioners Hope Schiele, Albert McLean and Frank L. Low filed a petition alleging that the company had liabilities of $183,388 and assets of less than $75,000. Doyle was the attorney for the petitioners and Conrad for the mortgage company.

Cravens and his attorneys arrived back in Kansas City October 5 from Omaha at the United States Court of Appeals where they had argued for a reversal of Cravens' and Alice B. Todd's conviction in 1928 in federal court. The appeals court in St. Louis decided the case November 28, 1932, and sent their decision on to Kansas City that day.

The defendants' appeal claimed their constitutional rights were violated by an unlawful search and seizure of property of the bank. To which the appeals court said no, that none of the material in question that was taken during the daring "midnight" raid in April 1927 by armed agents of the Treasury Department was used in the indictments. And even if they had been used, the opinion said, that would not have been material in the case as long as there was competent additional evidence on which to base the indictment.

As to court error in empaneling the jury, the appeals judges said, "We are unable to find reversible error in the order of the court nor in the way the order was carried out." Where the court was accused of "packing" the jury by the government, the opinion read that, "The mere fact that jurors are summoned by the marshal and paid by the government does not make them 'government men' on the jury."

The defendants claimed that the District Court committed reversible error when it forced Miss Todd to declare whether some of her entries in the Land Bank's financial records were false because that called for a conclusion, thus invading the province of the jury. And, further, by forcing Miss Todd to so answer forced her to incriminate herself in violation of the Fifth Amendment. To this, the appeals judges pointed out that she had already taken the witness stand in her own behalf and thus waived her immunity under the Fifth Amendment. The appeals court said about her being forced to declare entries in the bank's books as false, "We do not deem this question of much importance. She had fully and in detail explained all the facts and circumstances and had put her own interpretation upon the term 'false' as used by her."

The court said it had some sympathy with the argument by the defendants that the jury was necessarily confused by the multiplicity of counts, that a great deal of the evidence dealt with the intricate bank affairs and made difficult an intelligent understanding of every count. The court concluded, however, that confusion of the jury was no grounds for reversal.

The court affirmed 85 of the 88 counts of misapplication of funds and false entries in the bank's books with intent to defraud and deceive.

"While Walter Cravens was the controlling personage in the management of the land bank, the evidence is convincing that Miss Todd occupied a prominent place and was active in its management. She exhibited a remarkable carelessness in looking after the funds of the bank. Her own evidence shows her far from guiltless."

Judge William S. Kenyon wrote the court's opinion with Judge Archibald K. Gardner and Judge John B. Sanborn concurring.

"It is a shock," Walter Cravens told the Kansas City *Times* about the outcome of the appeal in his office in the Commerce Building. "We were confident the result would be a reversal."

Henry Conrad, who defended both Miss Todd and Cravens in the original trial and in their appeal, said he did not know where Miss

Todd was and wasn't even sure whether she would communicate with him. He indicated that a rehearing would be asked for in Cravens' case and that it could be referred to the Supreme Court if proper grounds were found.

Miss Todd's sister Anna's husband, Arch Taylor, said in Salina that she was in Kansas City. Both she and Cravens had thirty days to surrender and begin their prison terms, he at Leavenworth and Miss Todd at the institution for women in Alderson, West Virginia.

In early December in Salina, Miss Todd blamed her conviction on the fact that she was unable to get a separate trial. She said that the indictments that led her and Cravens to federal court in 1928 were the result of a contract entered into by the land bank and the Missouri Hydro-Electric Power Company without the approval of the Federal Farm Loan Board. This was done, she said, even though she had insisted that such approval be obtained. She felt that the defense counsel's refusal to obtain a separate trial for her in which she would have been able to introduce evidence she was unable to do with Cravens as a co-defendant, led to her conviction. The trial itself, she said, was conducted fairly and impartially and she had expected the appeals court to uphold the convictions. She said she would fight no further and was ready to serve her sentence of a year and a day. On December 16, she filed two more suits against Cravens, this time in the United States District Court.

The two new suits were similar to the ones already on the circuit court docket in Jackson County. In one of the suits Miss Todd sought $81,740 ($993,141) for one-fourth share of the settlement Walter Cravens received from Union Electric Light and Power Company and for money she says she loaned to Cravens.

Brother-in-law and attorney, Arch Taylor, represented Miss Todd when she filed her suit in December, 1932, as a resident of the state of Kansas, against Walter Cravens.

The suit contained three counts. Count 1 claimed Cravens owed her $22,200 ($270,840) for loans she had made him from her salary and direct amounts furnished, "to said defendant to be used in promoting a joint or partnership enterprise for the development of hydro-electric power on the Osage River at Bagnell, Missouri."

In consideration for the money she furnished him, Miss Todd said Cravens, "Orally agreed to pay all costs and expenses in the promotion of said enterprise and to turn over, pay and deliver to said plaintiff twenty-five percent of all moneys received by them growing out of said hydro-electric enterprise."

The petition went on to claim twenty-five percent of the $300,000 she claimed Cravens received from Union Electric Light and Power Company along with twenty-five percent of the rents and profits from the real estate Cravens had purchased with the money plus interest on the $75,000 due her.

In her second cause of action, she sought return of $5740 Cravens still owed her on the $6040 she had loaned to him during 1927, plus the interest.

Count Three covered the $1000 salary Cravens had orally promised her for representing him in the buying and selling of real estate in Minneapolis during 1930.

In January,1933, Miss Todd amended her petition to delete the part about the Kansas City real estate Cravens was alleged to have purchased with the money he received from Union Electric.

Henry Conrad lost no time in filing an answer to Miss Todd's petition. In addition to denying all her claims for money she said Cravens owed her, she actually, Conrad's motion to strike and dismiss said, owed Cravens $7500. To which Miss Todd, through her attorney on April 29, "denies each, every and all the allegations therein."

Cravens, now bombarded with claims from Miss Todd, Case 8662, and Wakefield and Muir, Case 8663, plus a prison sentence hanging over him, still fired back at his adversaries.

On January 7, 1933, he lost another battle with the federal court system when Samuel M. Carmean, assistant United States district attorney, announced that the Circuit Court of Appeals had denied Cravens a rehearing on its recent affirmation of his original conviction.

Alice B. Todd had not requested a rehearing, having said she would no longer fight her conviction.

Henry Conrad said, "Although I have not talked to my client, we probably will appeal to the United States Supreme Court."

He confirmed that two weeks later when he announced that Cravens would appeal. Miss Todd did not appeal, instead, seven days before she was to begin her prison sentence on February 27, she received news that made what she called, "one of the happiest days of my life." Judge Merrill Otis declared she had suffered enough during the five years spent with the shadow hanging over her. He placed her on two years of probation instead of the year and a day in prison.

"Generally speaking," said the same judge who had passed sentence on her that started the five year shadow, "probation is and should be granted only in that case in which the defendant being charged with a crime confesses his guilt, manifests sorrow and repentance for the offense and asks leniency."

"Repentance is too late," he said, 'after the government has gone to the expense and time of a trial. But, there are exceptions to all rules. Miss Todd was not the principal offender here. She is not responsible for the almost unprecedented delay and slowness with which the law and justice have moved in this case. That very delay has meant grievous punishment for her. I think she has been punished enough."

The judge said his view was shared by Roscoe C. Patterson, now a senator, who had prosecuted the case. Afterwards, Miss Todd said she would make her home in Salina, her, "old home town." She said she intended to pursue her lawsuits against her old boss, Walter Cravens.

On April 10, the United States Supreme Court denied Cravens' application for a review. Cravens asked for a ninety-day stay following his appeal to President Franklin D. Roosevelt, which was denied by the Justice Department. U.S. Marshal Asa Butler sent a deputy to find Cravens to serve formal papers committing him to Leavenworth prison. Deputy James H. Chandler went to Cravens' real estate office at 601 Commerce to inform him he was to report to prison, but was told Cravens had not been in the office that day. Chandler left orders that Cravens should surrender at the marshal's office by the next day or a search would begin for him. On May 17, 1933, Cravens surrendered and began his six-year prison term.

By this time, even Cravens' attempts to delay or quash the suits by Miss Todd and Wakefield against him began to run out of fuel. He had filed answers, motions, demurs and letters to the court claiming (1) Muir could not be a plaintiff in the case because he was not a resident in a state different from Cravens; (2) Muir had not signed onto the case as a plaintiff because he had sold out his interest in Cravens' note to Wakefield; (3) The $4000 loan had actually been paid to Alice B. Todd and not to him; (4) Wakefield and Muir had tried to injure the Hartley Company and Cravens with their involuntary bankruptcy suit; (5) there had actually been security given to Wakefield and Muir in the form of stock in the Campbell Harvey Underwriting Company and in the title to a property in Linn Creek; (6) the Federal District Court lacked jurisdiction in the case because none of the notes amounted to the requirement of $3000 for a civil case in the court.

The court and Judge Albert Reeves said no to all of those claims. Muir was a citizen of Kansas when the case was filed, his name was not required to be on the petition, The $4000, though it was received by Alice B. Todd, Cravens used it in his defense in the government's trial against him and Miss Todd and he had agreed that he would pay for the all of the expense of the criminal trial. The stock in the Campbell Harvey Underwriting Company had been returned to Cravens because he needed to sell the stock to get further cash for his and Miss Todd's defense. The Linn Creek property was sold and the money turned over to the mortgage company who held the note on it.

On February 13, 1934, Alice B. Todd filed a petition to the court dropping the first count in her petition against Cravens, the one in which she stated Cravens owed her twenty-five percent of the $300,000 received from Union Electric. Whether this indicated a settlement between her and Cravens is unknown.

On March 5, 1934, judgment was entered in the Federal District court by Judge Reeves against Walter Cravens for the amount of ($6028.37) ($73,546.11). But Cravens' creditors now ran into a new stumbling block. He was in prison and in the words of Judge Albert Reeves, "his civil rights are suspended and for the time being he is in effect civilly dead." This after Wakefield appealed to the court to have the defendant appear before the court and be examined as to his holdings that, Wakefield claimed under oath, to be, "in a large amount, but secretly held and in the possession of other parties whose names are unknown to the plaintiff."

Wakefield even wrote the judge and stated that he was, "at a loss how to proceed." He wrote the judge that, "it has been his (Cravens') fixed purpose to avoid payment and it has been the practice of his attorneys to use every delay to this end."

While in prison, even more reversals visited Cravens. In February 1934, the property he had purchased at 1116 Baltimore for $150,000 ($1,822,500) was foreclosed on by the former Federal Reserve Bank governor to satisfy a $75,000 mortgage held on the property. For Cravens, the mortgage bug had come full circle. The Baltimore property had been sold on the courthouse steps to salvage the mortgage.

Another investment Cravens had entered into did not work out for him; he was a silent angel in a bid to rehabilitate the General Utilities Company. Further proof that his business acumen had deserted him. Cravens never said how much the settlement from his involvement in the Missouri Hydro-Electric Company, variously reported to be as much as $350,000 ($4,252,500)—the base Alice B. Todd was claiming in court should have been shared with her—but denied it was the amount reported. The net amount was a lot less, he said. He had obligations to meet.

Meanwhile, his now seven-year fight for freedom was far from over. On June 4, 1935, Miss Josephine Myers, a Kansas City attorney, began talks with Department of Justice officials and Senator Harry S.

Truman, again concerning a Presidential pardon. No action was taken on Cravens' application.

Under regulations of Leavenworth prison and rules of the Justice Department, Cravens was eligible for parole after serving one-third of his sentence. Friends of Cravens were reported to be interceding on his behalf for a pardon or parole. Cravens immediately filed for parole as soon as his one-third sentence was completed. Henry Conrad said that attorneys in Washington D.C. were handling Cravens parole petition and he did not know what actions they were taking.

"He deserves to be paroled," Conrad said. "He is eligible for parole and I hope he gets it."

Nugent Dodds said he was doing nothing for Cravens parole, but that if the government asked him, he would make a recommendation. In July 1935, the federal board of pardons and paroles announced that it was considering Cravens application for a parole. Sanford Bates, director of federal prisons said that the Cravens case had been continued for further study by the board in Washington. In November the parole was denied. Cravens would remain in the Leavenworth prison until February 1937 when, three years and nine months after he entered incarceration, his request for parole was granted. The Department of Justice also announced a stay of execution on the $25,000 fine that had been levied against him. The records in the Department of Justice failed to reveal Cravens' sponsor.

Henry Conrad, Cravens' long-time attorney who specialized in keeping errant bankers out of jail, failed with Cravens, though Conrad would tell associates that he had a better defense for Cravens than he had for any of the others. "Walter Cravens," he said, "was the least cooperative defendant I ever knew."

In April, 1940, the Federal District Court received a request from Wakefield for garnishment from Cravens' insurance companies, Aetna and Travelers. This was granted and served to the State Superintendent of Insurance. U.S. Marshal Henry Dillingham certified that he made a diligent search throughout the Central Division and the Western District of Missouri and failed to find any property of any nature whatsoever belonging to Walter Cravens upon which to levy.

Walter Cravens, by this time, had returned to Kansas City to engage in business ventures, Ralph Street had resumed his law practice and Alice B. Todd had disappeared. Forever.

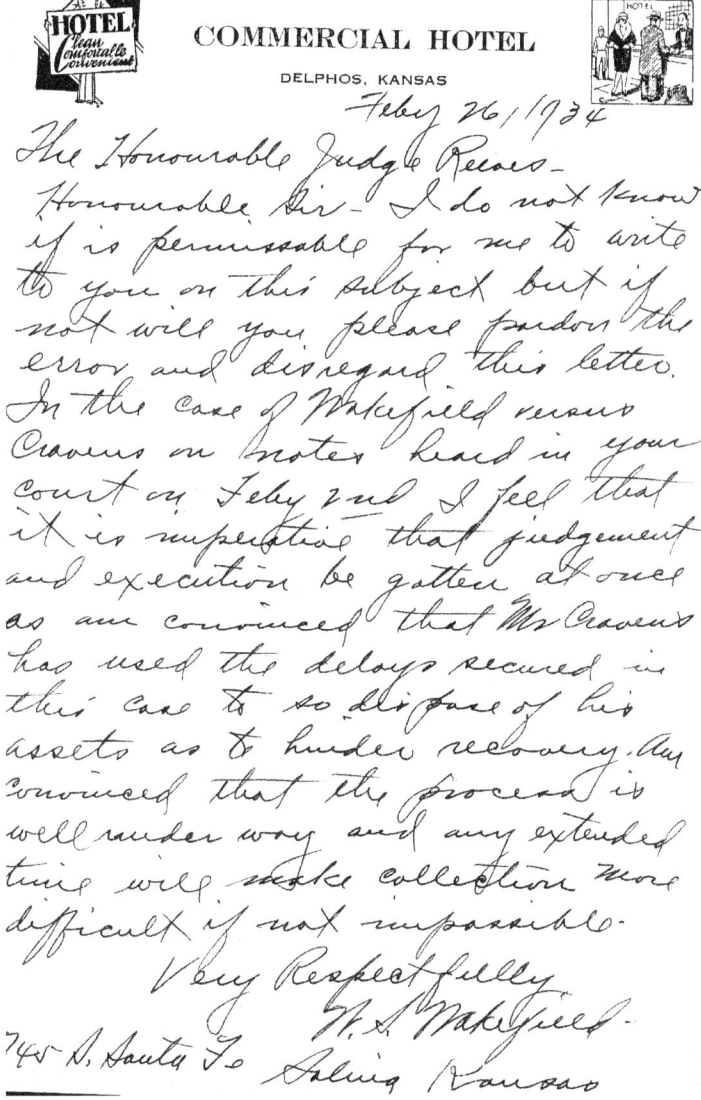

COMMERCIAL HOTEL
DELPHOS, KANSAS

Feby 26, 1934

The Honourable Judge Reees —
Honourable Sir — I do not know if is permissable for me to write to you on this subject but if not will you please pardon the error and disregard this letter. In the case of Wakefield versus Cravens on notes heard in your court on Feby 2nd I feel that it is imperative that judgement and execution be gotten at once as am convinced that Mr Cravens has used the delays secured in this case to so dispose of his assets as to hinder recovery. Am convinced that the process is well under way and any extended time will make collection more difficult if not impossible.

Very Respectfully
W. A. Wakefield.
745 N. Santa Fe   Salina Kansas

EPILOGUE

On May 26, 1943, a woman appeared at the Social Security office in Mora, Minnesota, to apply for a Social Security number. She signed her application as Barbara Todd. On the form she wrote that she had been born with the name of Alice Barbara Todd. It was, of course, the same Alice B. Todd who had been convicted fifteen years earlier in the infamous Kansas City Joint Stock Land Bank trial. The following obituary appeared in the Salina, Kansas, *Journal* October 18, 1971:

> BARBARA A. TODD
>
> The funeral for Barbara Alice Todd, 86, 745 S. Santa Fe, a retired secretary and office manager, will be at 2 pm Tuesday at the First Presbyterian Church, Dr. Bernard Hawley officiating.
>
> Miss Todd, whose career in Civil Service took her to such projects as the Alcan Highway in Alaska and the atomic energy installation at Oak Ridge, Tenn. Died Sunday at Asbury hospital where she had been a patient 3 days.
>
> She was born in Saline County Feb. 4, 1885 and returned to Salina in 1949 after working in Civil Service. For many years, she lived in Kansas City, MO. Until retirement she was associated with the Red Cross and Shellabarger Mills here.
>
> She was a Presbyterian.
>
> Surviving are 3 nieces and a nephew.
>
> Friends may call at the Rush Smith funeral home until Tuesday noon. The casket will remain closed at the church. Burial will be in Gypsum Hill Cemetery.

The Salina *Journal* reported this notice on May 11, 1946.

MRS BERTHA CRAVENS

Mrs Walter Cravens, the former Bertha Hoover of Salina, sister of the late S.E. Hoover and aunt of Warren Hoover, 906 West Ash, died Friday morning in Chicago. Details of the funeral were not known to relatives here today, but her daughters, Mrs Virginia Slater and Miss Frances Cravens, indicated in telephone conversation with Mr. Hoover late Friday that burial may be in Salina in the family plot in Gypsum Hill Cemetery.

On November 11, 1968, the Salina Journal carried this obituary:

WALTER P. CRAVENS

Funeral arrangements for Walter P. Cravens, 86, Kansas City, MO, a former Salina resident, are pending at the Rush Smith funeral home. Burial will be in the Gypsum Hill Cemetery. Mr. Cravens died Tuesday after a lengthy illness. He was born April 11, 1882, in Salina. He was the son of Mr. and Mrs. R.P. Cravens, who came to Salina in 1878 after Mr. Cravens graduated from the Columbia, Mo. Law School.

Walter attended school in Salina and moved to Kansas City Mo., in 1918, where he has lived since. He was a retired investment-businessman.

He was a member of the Christian Church, Masons, Consistory and Isis Shrine.

Survivors include his mother, Mrs. R.P. Cravens, 715 S. Santa Fe; the widow, Josephine of the home; two daughters, Mrs. John Slater, San

Francisco, Calif., and Frances Cravens, Washington, D.C., and three brothers, Kenton, St. Louis, Mo., Rolland, Los Angeles, Calif., and Jewell, Martha's Vineyard, Conn.

Friends may call at the funeral home.

On May 16, 1953, the Kansas City *Times* recorded this obituary:

RALPH W. STREET Dies
LAWYER, 70, HAD HEADED MISSOURI SONS OF REVOLUTION
He Was Credited With Conceiving the construction of Bagnell
dam which formed the
Lake of the Ozarks

Ralph Wood Street, 70, lawyer, who was credited with the conception of the Bagnell Dam which resulted in the Lake of the Ozarks, died last night at the home, 6444 Summit street, after an illness of three years.

Mr. Street was born in St. Joseph, Mo., and had been a resident of Kansas City thirty-eight years. He was graduated from the law school of the University of Michigan, and practiced here since that time except for a brief period in St. Joseph. He had limited his practice since his illness, but maintained offices at 1016 Baltimore Avenue.

Mr. Street was a member of the Presbyterian church. He was president of the Missouri Society of the Sons of the Revolution in 1950 and had served several times as a member of the board of governors of the organization. He was a member of the Lawyers association and Phi Gamma Delta social fraternity.

In 1923 Mr. Street began to map and plan the promotion of the big hydroelectric project shortly after a trip through the Bagnell territory. The dam was completed in 1930.

His wife, Mrs. Alice Brown Street of the home survives

The Ithaca, NY Journal on September 30, 1961 carried this article about George Jessup, superintendent of construction at Bagnell Dam for Stone & Webster:

G.P. Jessup Dies at 77

George P. Jessup Sr., 77 project engineer in the department of Buildings and Properties at Cornell University died Friday, Sept. 29, 1961, in the Tompkins County Hospital.

A graduate of the College of Mechanical Engineering at Cornell in 1908, he worked for British and Canadian engineering firms in Canada in World War I, ans an employee of the eigineering firm of Stone and Webster of Boston, Mass., he supervised the sonstruction of Army munitions warehouses for the U.S. government near Dijon, France.

After the war, he was superintendent of hydro-electric projects including the xconstruction of a dam and powerhouse for Henry Ford on the Menominee river at Iron Mountain, MIch.,for the Puget Sound Power and Light Co. on the Baker River, Concrete, Wash., and for Union electric Co., on the Osage River at Bagnell, Mo. . . . .

Mr. Jessup is survived by his wife, Mrs. Mannie Dealy Jessup' a sister, Mrs. William H. Wilson of Noyac, Sag Harbor; a son, George P. Jessup Jr. of Panama City, Fla.; three daughters, Mrs. Thomas G. McCawley of Webster Groves, Mo., Mrs. Boret H. Underwood of Manchester, Tenn., and Mrs. Jan R. Beaujon of Cincinnati, O., and 12 grandchildren.

Alice B. Todd, one time Kansas City's most celebrated female executives and one of only two females executives in the nation in federal land banks, and a convicted felon for falsifying land bank records, ended her life as Barbara Alice Todd, a retired and accomplished secretary and office manager in Civil Service. It is significant that neither Miss Todd's obituary nor Walter Cravens' made mention of their part in building Bagnell Dam and creating the Lake of the Ozarks. Ralph Street alone, of the three, got recognition for that accomplishment. Henry Conrad, the lawyer, told that Street had said at one time, "Of all the things I have ever done in my life, this is my baby, this hydro project."

It still remains unknown in the official records what settlement Miss Todd may have received from Walter Cravens for the sale of the dam to Union Electric, if any, but she did at least have the satisfaction of outliving him.

AmerenUE, who took over Union Electric Light and Power Company, contains in their records the name of every employee of that company who worked for them in the construction.

Stone & Webster, long considered the preeminent engineering company in the country, ran into financial and finally, legal problems in the 1990's and filed for bankruptcy. They became part of the Shaw Group. In 1996 Stone & Webster landed a "bet-the-company project," a $950 million deal to construct an integrated ethylene and olefins complex in Indonesia, for a company known as Trans-Pacific Petrochemical Indotama, or TPPI. The catch was, according to the report by Baker & McKenzie: the demand by the project's owner, a relative of President Suharto for a kickback equal to about 15 percent of the project's cost, or $147 million.

The shareholders who came after those involved with the failure of the Indonesian project, lost everything. Stone & Webster's stock market value sank from $590 million in January 1998 to next to nothing by mid-May, when the company filed for bankruptcy court protection. The project was eventually built by the Shaw Group, who bought Stone & Webster's assets. Stone & Webster's employees, on the other hand, lost not only their jobs, but much of their retirement savings. The final bill: about $123 million in company stock in their 401(k) and employee stock ownership plans.

Union Electric and their parent holding company, the North American Company had their legal problems in the 30's. Quoting an article in *Time* magazine's July 29, 1940 issue:

> "The problems," came from St. Louis, where the $257,000,000 Union Electric Co., one of North American's crack subsidiaries, earned for North American about $6,000,000 a year.
>
> Across the street from Union Electric on Twelfth Boulevard stands the St. Louis *Post-Dispatch*, the great Pulitzer newspaper whose mission is policing the community. P-D's public-utility reporter, a thin-haired A. E. F. sergeant named Sam Shelton, had long been convinced that Union Electric was buying politicians.
>
> Two years ago he got a break when Union Electric's moose-tall aristocratic president Louis H. Egan eased out a vice president named Oscar Funk. Funk, who had handled Union Electric's expense accounts, knew where more bodies were buried than a Nazi concentration-camp keeper. Shelton went after him, got his story, and scampered to SEC.
>
> SEC began a secret investigation, and Sam Shelton began a series of exclusive stories that kept P-D readers in a state of mixed rage and amusement. From testimony in trials that resulted it appeared that: Union Electric's Lobbyist Albert Laun and his friends had developed a slush fund of at least $525,000 which never appeared on Union Electric's books.

One company lawyer had kicked back $111,000 in excess fees; another $42,000; a Kansas City equipment salesman had kicked back $70,000; insurance companies had refunded $80,000. This money then went into the campaign funds of candidates for every office in Union Electric's territory from alderman to Governor of Missouri."

Laun,' reported Shelton,' kept his list of bribes under a carpet in his office. On information supplied by SEC, Al Laun went to Leavenworth three months ago, and Frank Boehm, formerly executive vice president, is now on trial for perjury in Federal court. Since the SEC hearings began, Union Electric's Missouri tax assessments have been upped 27%.

As these disclosures popped, North American, first replaced (but kept on salary) Union Electric Officers Egan ($58,000), Boehm ($41,000), and Laun ($16,800). Few months later, all three resigned and two other officers were demoted."

According to articles in the *Post Dispatch,* Laun, Egan and other top Union Electric officials provided lavish entertainment of legislators and other public officials in the Red Arrow Lodge on the Big Niangua arm and in the administration lodge once called Egan's Lodge, now known as Willmore Lodge. The direct and indirect campaign contributions approved by Egan and other top Union Electric officials were felonious violations of the federal Holding Company Act, the SEC said.

In 1941 Union Electric put the lodge up for sale after Laun and Vice President Frank Boehm had been convicted of perjury in the SEC investigation. Egan and the company were indicted for violating the Holding Company Act.

In 1943 an enormous flood hit the Midwest causing the lake level to overflow the dam. In the 1970's, Truman Dam was built upstream on the Osage River near the town of Warsaw in Benton County which curtailed recent floods from overflowing the dam.

Louis Egan, Union Electric's president when the dam was built, predicted a great tourist attraction for the Lake of the Ozarks. His prediction was vastly under estimated. Latest statistics telling the popularity of the Lake prior to publication stated an estimated four and one half million visitors to the area each year. The Lake Area Chamber of Commerce gave population figures of 40,664 for Camden County and 24,949 for Miller County. Lake Ozark, the fastest growing town in the four county area, saw an increase of 37 percent since 2000. Sales tax figures for 2009 for the city of Osage Beach was $4,254,000 and $1,392,000 for Camdenton. An estimated 40,000 to 50,000 boats use the Lake during a year's time. More than 250 individual condominium complexes are located in the four county area with an estimated 100 units per project, mostly populated by weekend visitors.

Union Electric Light and Power Company is now part of AmerenUE. The Osage Plant at Bagnell Dam is used primarily as back-up for seasonal peak periods.

ACKNOWLEDGMENTS

Information for DAM OVER TROUBLED WATERS referenced the following documents:

NEWSPAPERS AND MAGAZINES

The Kansas City *Star* and the Kansas City *Times*, Kansas City, Missouri

The *Reveille*, Linn Creek, Missouri

The St. Louis *Globe-Democrat*, St. Louis, Missouri.

The St. Louis *Post-Dispatch*, St. Louis, Missouri.

The Springfield *Daily News*, Springfield, Missouri.

The Jefferson City *Post Tribune*, Jefferson City, Missouri

The Kansas City *Journal-Post*, Kansas City, Missouri

The Miller County *Autogram*, Tuscumbia, Missouri

The Versailles *Statesman*, Versailles, Missouri

The Eldon *Advertiser*, Eldon, Missouri

New York *Journal of Commerce*, New York, NY

The Boston *Globe*, Boston, MA

The Ithaca *Journal*, Ithaca, NY

Time Magazine

Missouri Ruralist

BOOKS

Kansas City and Its One Hundred Foremost Men, Walter P. Tracy

Financial Study of the Joint Stock Land Banks: A Study in the Farm Mortgage Banking, Carl Herbert Schwartz

Before the Dam Waters, T. Victor Jeffries

The Story of Bagnell Dam, Carole Tellman Pilkington

A Town On Two Rivers, Victoria Hubbell

The Art of Speculation, Philip L Carret

Banking Principles and Practice, Ray B. Westerfield

Stone & Webster, 1889-1999: A Century of Integrity and Service, David Neal Keller

A Standard History of Kansas and Kansans, William Elsey Connelley

The Federal Reporter, 1933, West Publications

Sons of the Revolution, Missouri Society, 1909 Yearbook

FEDERAL PUBLICATIONS

United States Department of the Interior, National Park Service, National Register of Historic Places, Land Bank Building, Kansas City, Missouri

Annual Report, Federal Farm Loan Board, 1931

Proceedings of Federal District Court, Western Division, National Archives, Case Numbers 233, 1365, 7508, 7564, 7957, 8002, 8662, 8663, 9235 (Federal Appeals Court)

Congressional Hearing Committee on Banking and Currency, U.S. House of Representatives, 71st Congress, HR9433

MISSOURI STATE PUBLICATIONS:

Minutes of Public Service Commission Hearings, Case Numbers 4632 and 6474

OTHER PUBLICATIONS:

Missouri Valley Special Collection, Kansas City, Missouri Public Library

Missouri Bar Association Journal, 1931

AmerenUE History of Bagnell Dam, Compiled by William E. Turner

Minutes of Camden County Court, 1926-1931

INDIVIDUALS: This book would not have been possible without the assistance of the following. My sincere thanks to everyone of them.

Kaitlyn Mcbride, student, for her help in finding Barbara Alice Todd.

Jessica Edgar and Sarah Ford for their assistance at the National Archives in Kansas City.

Debbie Steck at the Missouri Public Service Commission for her assistance with commission documents.

Elaine McClymonds of Stone & Webster.

Alan Sullivan of AmerenUE.

Krys Reese of the Kansas City *Star.*

www.ingramcontent.com/pod-product-compliance
Lightning Source LLC
Chambersburg PA
CBHW051121160426
43195CB00014B/2295